W9-BNI-949

THE SIMON & SCHUSTER POCKET GUIDE TO

HOME SEWING

BY ANN LADBURY

The Simon & Schuster Pocket Guide to Home Sewing

A Fireside Book
Published by Simon & Schuster Inc.
New York London Toronto Sydney Tokyo

THE SIMON & SCHUSTER POCKET GUIDE TO HOME SEWING
BY ANN LADBURY

Copyright © Mitchell Beazley Publishers 1988
Text copyright © Ann Ladbury 1988
Illustrations copyright © Ann Ladbury and Mitchell Beazley
Publishers 1988

A Fireside Book, published by Simon & Schuster Inc.
Simon & Schuster Building, Rockefeller Center
1230 Avenue of the Americas, New York, New York 10020

FIRESIDE and colophon are registered trademarks of Simon &
Schuster Inc.

Edited and designed by Mitchell Beazley International Ltd.
Artists House, 14–15 Manette Street, London W1V 5LB

Editor	Maggie Ramsay
Art Editor	Jill Raphaeline
Illustrations	Ann Ladbury
Executive Editor	Bob Saxton
Production	Barbara Hind

Originally published in Great Britain by Mitchell Beazley Publishers
under the title The Simplicity® Pocket Guide to Home Sewing.

Typeset by Bookworm Typesetting, Manchester
Colour reproduction by David Bruce Graphics Ltd
Printed and bound in Hong Kong by Mandarin Offset

Library of Congress Catalog Card Number: 87-32947

ISBN: 0-671-64234-0

The following brand names are trademarks in the USA: Fray
Check®; Waist-Shaper®; Stitch Witchery® (USM Corporation);
Wonder-Under™, Stitch-n-Tear®, Fold-a-Band™, Wonder-
Web™, Pellon® (Freudenberg Nonwoven Limited Partnership,
Pellon Division); VELCRO®, VELCOIN® (both owned by Velcro
USA Inc.).

The following brand names are trademarks in the UK: Poppa
Snaps®, Velcro®, Wunderweb®, Vilene®, Bondaweb®.
Fold-a-Band and Stitch-n-Tear are Vilene® products. Spot-Ons are
a Velcro® product.

CONTENTS

INTRODUCTION

This book is about how to repair and care for your clothes. In times past most people felt obliged to try to make mending invisible, partly to avoid being thought unable to afford to buy new things. In addition, painfully small stitching was regarded as virtuous. These days we take a more realistic view and we even applaud those who are thrifty and repair their clothes. There is no longer any need to be expert in stitchery; a young man who has patched his own jeans, albeit with big stitches and contrasting thick yarn, will be admired for not expecting a woman to do it for him. In fact, there is such a wide range of aids available that require only to be pressed in place with the iron that he, and you, can avoid actual sewing altogether.

Fashion has also come to our aid. Bright patches, gaudy inserts and bold appliqués in odd places are perfectly acceptable, and all these things can conceal a hole or damaged area. So do not despair if you have an accident. A friend of mine got a blot of ink on the bodice of a brand new party dress. Wiping the tears away, she embroidered a bold flower over the blot and then repeated the flower all over the bodice before she wore the dress again. Everyone wanted to know where she bought it.

In this book you will find a variety of techniques that need very little skill. Previous experience is not essential; beginners of all ages, male and female, will be able to follow the instructions.

And if you are one of those who 'can't thread a needle', well, read on and learn how.

KEY TO DRAWINGS

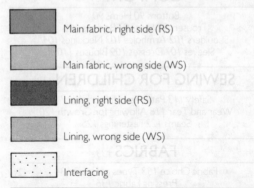

Main fabric, right side (RS)

Main fabric, wrong side (WS)

Lining, right side (RS)

Lining, wrong side (WS)

Interfacing

American equivalents are given in this book for both sewing terms and brand names. The alternatives are separated by an oblique stroke, like this: UK/US.

BASICS

SEWING EQUIPMENT

Some items will already exist in the household so you may only need to add a few more. If you are starting from scratch, buy, beg or borrow what you need. Start at the top of the list; they are in order of necessity, although in the end you will find they are all useful and make sewing easier.

Needles. You will need **ordinary** sewing needles, betweens or sharps, for stitching by hand. A **darning** needle, long and sharp with a big eye, and a **tapestry** or **knitters'** needle, short and blunt with a big eye, will also be useful for thick threads and knitting yarn. A needle for **leather**, with a sharp wedge point which makes a three point cut, is for sewing buttons and stitching on leather. A **crewel** needle, with a long eye for embroidery thread and floss, might come in handy.

Threads. For machine stitching and hand sewing.
   Collect reels/spools of core-spun/cotton-wrapped polyester, mercerized and cotton thread in black, white, cream, navy and other shades as you need them.
   Heavy duty, **linen** and **button** thread will be useful for sewing on buttons and repairs on heavy articles.

Scissors. Have a small pair with short sharp points for snipping thread and a large pair with handles that are comfortable to grip for cutting fabric.

Unpicker/seam ripper. One of these may be included with sewing machine accessories but it will probably be small and difficult to hold. Buy one with a large handle. Unpickers/seam rippers can be dangerous; keep the top on and keep hidden from children.

Iron. You will need an iron for the many fusible sewing and repair products available and also for pressing your completed alteration or repair. The heat of the iron will help embed the stitches as well as smooth the fabric. If a steam iron is not available use a damp pressing cloth or well-wrung handkerchief under the iron.
   Also, make sure you have an **iron cleaner** – used to remove marks and adhesive from the base of the iron.

Elastic threader. Also used for threading cord etc., this has a very large rectangular eye. For threading a long cord or elastic or for threading ribbon through slots a **rouleau needle/ball end bodkin** is easier to use. This is a long needle with a large eye and a ball at the opposite end.

Beeswax. Very useful for rubbing along polyester thread when it snarls or twists when hand stitching. Also used for lubricating zipper teeth after dry-cleaning or laundering. Beeswax is also essential for waxing thread when attaching buttons.

Marking pen. A special felt-tip pen for making marks on fabric as guides for stitching, placing or matching up edges. A very valuable sewing aid, especially the type that makes marks that fade automatically, without the need for water.

Measuring gauge and tape measure. The gauge is a short metal or plastic rule with a movable marker that can be set to a specific measurement. It is useful because it is rigid and helps eliminate errors when the same measurement is required more than once.

Use a tape measure for longer measurements, for curves and shapes and for measuring the body.

Pins. It is worth obtaining dressmakers' steel pins, either the conventional shape or those with plastic heads. They pierce more easily than cheaper pins and they do not mark fabric. Plastic knitters' pins and ball point pins may be useful on knitting and knit fabrics but are not essential.

Tweezerbodkin. A useful tool comprising tweezers at one end for removing odd ends of thread and a point at the other for loosening stitches, removing basting stitches, easing out corners, points and ends of belts.

Crochet hook. A small crochet hook is useful for picking up loops in knitting and for repairing runs in knit fabrics.

Sewing machine. Although nearly all repairs can be made using hand stitching and fusible products, machine stitching is better for renovations and replacements and where long seams or large areas of fabric are involved.

A machine with basic straight and zigzag facilities is adequate for the techniques in this book but if you have access to a more sophisticated model you will be able to make use of decorative stitches as well.

Thimble. Although this item is last on the list it is not because it is least important. If you have a full set of sewing tools your thimble will be among them and you will know its value. Let me say to the beginners, by the time you have used this book to sew on a few buttons, put a zipper in your jeans and sewn on one or more suede patches, you will very much *want* a thimble. Take my advice, and buy a tailor's thimble, the type with both ends open. It is much more comfortable to wear and if you hold the needle correctly it is the side of your middle finger that pushes against it, not the end.

SEWING AIDS

There are a number of products available that you will find useful. Buy them if and when you find you need them or borrow them from friends. There are other items sold specially for repair jobs and although I have referred to some of them in the book as being useful, they are, on the whole, expensive.

Basting tape. Narrow adhesive tape that can be used single or double-sided. Very useful for inserting zippers, holding patches etc. in position. Does not have to be removed if covered with fabric.

Chalk pencil. Use for making lines and matching points or marking spots on fabric, eg. position of button. Some pencils have a brush attached, although marks are easily removed.

Decorative snap fasteners, eg. Poppa-Snaps (UK). Solid fasteners to be attached to fabric using tool in pack. Metal or plastic caps snap on the outside of the article.

Fray Check (UK/US). Liquid that is explained by its name. A small amount applied to a worn or fraying edge of fabric will prolong its life. It also contains the fibres while you carry on stitching or handling the fabric.

Fusible waistband, eg. Fold-a-Band (UK/US)/**Waist-shaper.** Interfacing strip with central perforations; firm weight for waistbands and belts, soft strip for cuffs, tabs, bands, straps etc. A very useful aid that speeds things up and also reinforces the fabric.

Fusible web, eg. Wundaweb/Fabric Bond, Wonder-Web, Stitch Witchery. Use for holding hems and edges in place, for securing facings and for controlling fraying fabric. Place the web between two layers of fabric and press firmly using a hot iron and a damp pressing cloth. Make sure the web melts thoroughly.

Glue stick. Useful for anchoring patches etc. while you stitch. Can be messy if not covered but it washes out.

Hooks and eyes and snaps. Metal hooks and snaps are black or silver and are available in many sizes. Use small ones on fine fabric and for an inconspicuous fastening, large ones on heavy fabric or for a stronger fastening. They may be sewn in position with oversewing stitches through each hole, but you may find it worth while learning how to do buttonhole stitch because it is so much neater and more professional-looking.

Iron-on interfacing, eg. Vilene/Pellon. A non-woven

supporting material with adhesive that melts when ironed, making the interfacing adhere to the fabric. Various weights are available; the softest kind has a number of uses in repairs and renovations.

Paper-backed adhesive web, eg. Bondaweb/ Wonder-Under. This can be cut to shape, perhaps for a patch, pressed to the fabric using a hot iron and a damp cloth, then the paper backing peeled off. The fabric can then be placed on top of another, adhesive side down, and pressed again. No stitching is necessary and it will withstand washing.

Snaps on tape. These can be used instead of buttons and buttonholes or snaps, especially on a long opening. Attach by stitching along the edge of the tape with the machine zipper foot, or stitch by hand.

Tape-maker. A gadget for making and folding bias strips of fabric ready to use for binding, ties, straps etc. Available in various sizes. Cut bias strips of fabric to width specified on package, pressing the strip as you pull it from the tool.

Tear-away backing, eg. Stitch-n-Tear (UK/US). A non-woven material resembling parchment used underneath fabric to support it while embroidering by machine. It will also prevent missed stitches and wrinkled seams when used under soft fabrics such as crepe de Chine and silk or synthetic jersey.

Trouser clasps. These are flat hooks and bars that make a strong waistband fastening. For maximum strength they should be attached with tape which is passed through the the holes in the hook before being secured with stitching, but the alternative is to stitch round each hole of the hook using waxed double thread preferably with buttonhole stitch rather than oversewing.

Velcro fasteners. A useful substitute for buttons and snaps. Velcro fastener comes in strip form for long openings and in discs (Spot-On/Velcoin) for small openings or in place of buttonholes. Attach by oversewing around the edge or stitch by machine using a small zigzag stitch.

THINGS WORTH COLLECTING

The business of updating clothes will be more exciting and cheaper if you have a store of interesting bits and pieces to dip into. The following list suggests things you could snap up in thrift shops, sales, bargain counters and market stalls as well as when friends and relatives go through their wardrobes and clear things out. Snip off the item you need and dispose of the remainder of the garment.

1. Balls of knitting yarn.

2. Beaded or sequinned motifs and evening bags.

3. Beads; including jewellery as well as craft beads.

4. Bias binding.

5. Buckles and clasps in metal or plastic.

6. Buttons; especially in sets, or old buttons, shirt buttons, pearl buttons, men's coat buttons and small backing buttons.

7. Cord and braid of any kind.

8. Dungaree buckles and 'D' rings.

9. Earrings; wires from earrings for pierced ears can be re-used, clasps from clip-ons can be used for dress and shoe ornaments.

10. Elastic of all kinds; new only.

11. Fabrics that might be useful, either as pieces or as garments that can be cut up, include:

   – Any bargain price fabric that you particularly like.

   – Cottons in classic designs such as spots and stripes.

   – Fur and fur fabric, pieces and strips.

   – Glitter fabric.

   – Lace; collars, edging, motifs and pieces.

   – Lining fabrics; new only.

   – Needlecord and corduroy; make good patches as well as yokes etc.

   – Plain crepe de Chine for cutting into bias strips.

   – Suede and leather; even small pieces can be cut into strips and punched with holes to make decorative strips.

   – Suede fabric.

   – Wadding/batting of any kind.

12. Jet or diamanté/rhinestone trimming of any kind.

13. Metal eyelets.

14. Ribbons of all widths; avoid old and tatty specimens, but often new reels/spools and cards of ribbon can be found.

15. Sequins; often found still sealed in their original containers. Sequins in strip form are useful.

16. Shoulder pads; especially in foam or non-woven material.

17. Socks; tops can be used as cuff ribbing.

18. Zippers of all types, provided they run well.

HOW TO THREAD A NEEDLE

It is easier to use a small needle than a large one – a thick clumsy needle is difficult to push through the fabric.

Begin by selecting the thread or yarn to suit your fabric: sewing thread for neat repairs to woven fabric; thick wool to mend knitted things; strong thick thread where there is strain, eg. buttons. Next choose a needle with an eye just big enough for that thread to pass through.

Cut a length of thread not much longer than the distance from your hand to your elbow. Sometimes longer thread is needed for darning or for basting, but for normal sewing a long thread tends to become tangled and can be difficult to control.

Hold the needle in one hand and the thread in the other and sit down with your elbows on a table. Moisten the end of the thread, flattening it with your teeth. Rest your two wrists against each other **(1)** – and thread the needle! Still with your wrists together, take the needle in the other hand and pull the thread through. As you pull, form a knot by moving your finger so that the thread entwines it once. Rub your thumb towards the end of your forefinger **(2)** to make the knot. If the thread is required double, pull it through until both ends are even, then form the knot.

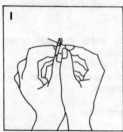
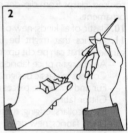

Soft thread. Some soft threads are difficult to flatten sufficiently to pass them through the eye of the needle. With these, wrap the end tightly around the needle to make a flat loop which will pass easily through the eye.

Needle threader. This is a useful tool which consists of a small metal disc with a wire loop attached. Push the wire loop into the eye of the needle. Pass end of thread through loop and withdraw wire to pull thread through eye.

STITCHES

Numbers in brackets refer to the diagrams, p. 13.

Backstitch (1). A strong stitch used for fastening off almost all hand stitches, for repairing seams and for small areas where machining might be awkward. The stitches should form a continuous row.

Work from right to left keeping stitches as small as possible, no more than ⅛in (3mm) on top of work. Stitches on WS are twice the length of those on top and look rather untidy. Start with a knot on WS, bring needle through to RS and insert ⅛in (3mm) behind knot. Bring out ⅛in (3mm) in front of this first stitch and insert where stitch ended on RS.

Half backstitch is neater, more attractive and stronger than ordinary backstitch, although still untidy on WS. The stitches do not form a continuous row; the space between them equals the length of the stitches – 1/16in (2mm). Suitable for places where full backstitch would produce too large a stitch, causing the fabric to part.

Work as for backstitch, but take needle back and through

WS only ¹⁄₁₆in (2mm) behind emerging thread. Bring up to RS ⅛in (3mm) in front of stitch as in backstitch. Pull thread tight with each stitch if working on a seam to ensure that the seam does not open up and show threads.

Basting (2). Used to hold two or more layers of fabric together or for marking single layers. Start with a knot on RS and work from right to left. Work on a flat surface. Push needle through fabric in one continuous in-and-out movement, making stitches about ¾in (2cm) long, shorter around curves or difficult areas. Pick up on needle as little fabric as possible between stitches – about ⅛in (3mm). If too much fabric is picked up, the layers of fabric part or the fabric moves when it is machined. Finish with one backstitch, or two if preparing for fitting. To remove, snip backstitch and pull starting knot gently.

Diagonal basting (3). A large stitch used to cover areas quickly. Keeps fabric flat, whereas ordinary basting would cause ridges. Particularly suitable for inserting interfacings and holding linings.

Work on RS, starting with a knot. Take a small horizontal stitch from right to left through fabric. Working toward you, take another stitch the same size as, and parallel to, the first. Do not pull thread tight or ridges will form. The length of the stitches varies according to the amount of control required. Take short stitches close together for greater control, longer ones more widely spaced if less control is needed. Several rows can be worked, about 1¼in (3cm) apart. Finish each with one loose backstitch.

Blanketstitch (4). Also called loopstitch. Sometimes confused with buttonhole stitch but less lumpy and a loop is made rather than a knot. The stitches can be close together or spaced out, depending on where they are used.

Work from left to right with edge toward you and start with a backstitch on WS. Bring needle and thread around to RS and insert needle above edge on RS, holding thread below edge. Bring needle out below edge over held thread. Settle thread so that it lies along edge. Still holding thread, take another stitch to the right.

Buttonhole stitch (5). Used for hand worked buttonholes, and also for finishing a short length of raw edge to prevent fraying. Difficult to work neatly because a knot is formed with each stitch and an even tension must be kept on all knots.

Begin with a knot or backstitch on WS and work toward you with cut edge to right (or left, if left-handed). Take thread over edge and insert needle point from WS beside knot. To form a knot, wind double section of thread by eye of needle around needle point toward you. Although the fingers should leave the needle at this stage, keep thimble in place at eye of needle to steady it while knot is formed. Let go of thread and finish pulling needle through fabric. To settle knot on edge of fabric, grasp thread near knot and tug it gently into position. Work next stitch beside it, nearer to you. The closeness of the stitches depends on the thickness of the thread, but keep spacing even and make sure that the knots touch.

Catch stitch (6). Used to hold up hems in medium and heavy fabrics, and sometimes over a raw edge in short lengths. Although weak, it is invisible on RS. It serves the same purpose as herringbone, but is neater. To avoid a ridge on hems, work stitch just under hem edge, ⅛–¼in (3–6mm) down, depending on thickness of fabric. If it is worked lower, the weight of the edge eventually pulls and makes a line.

Work from right to left. Fasten thread inside hem with a knot or backstitch. Take a very small stitch in hem fabric and, ⅛–¼in (3–6mm) to left, depending on thickness of fabric, a small stitch in garment.

Chain stitch (7). Although mainly an embroidery stitch, it has its uses in repairs and renovations. Start with a backstitch and bring thread through to RS. Make a small loop and insert needle at point where it emerged, holding loop out to a length of ¹⁄₁₆–⅛in (2–3mm). Bring needle out just inside end of this first loop and continue to form a chain. Fasten off by taking needle through last loop and working several backstitches on WS.

Cross stitch (8). Like chain stitch, this is mainly an embroidery stitch. The needle must be stabbed through the work with each movement. This makes the other side untidy, so use only inside a garment, eg. for linings and seam allowances.

Work from right to left. Start with a backstitch and bring needle through to RS. Insert needle vertically, making a series of equal sized diagonal stitches. To form a cross stitch, work from left to right, sewing back again over original stitches, inserting needle through the same holes.

Fishbone stitch (9). Also called lacing stitch. This is a loose chevron stitch which can be used for drawing edges together before permanent stitching is inserted.

Start with a backstitch; hold needle at a slant and take a series of stitches alternately to right and left. Do not pull thread tight. Finish with a backstitch.

Hemming stitch (10). A strong stitch, worked on WS to hold down a fold of fabric. It shows on RS and is therefore, despite its name, unsuitable for most hems.

Work toward you. Begin with a knot, on WS of edge if possible, but if working on sheer fabric start with a small

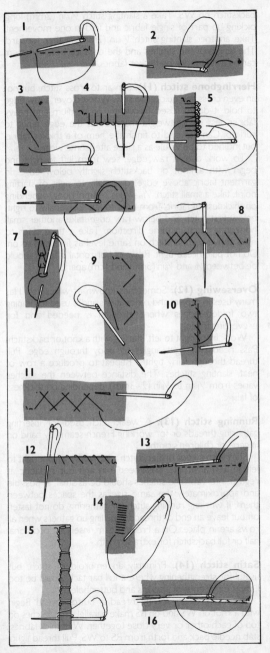

backstitch on WS. Take a slanting stitch 1/16in (2mm) long, picking up part of single fabric and fold in one movement. Take another slanting stitch 1/16in (2mm) farther forward. The length of the stitches and the distance between them can be a little more on thicker fabrics.

Herringbone stitch (11). Similar to cross stitch, but not an even cross and quicker to sew. Worked over a raw edge to hold it down. Used frequently on medium and heavy fabrics, less on lightweight materials as the edge tends to curl up. Can be used to finish the hem of a thicker fabric, but inclined to be visible as a ridge after some wear.

To work over a raw edge, sew from left to right and begin with a knot or backstitch slightly below edge. In garment fabric above edge, diagonally to right of starting point, take a small stitch, 1/16–1/8in (2–3mm) long, depending on thickness of fabric, from right to left. Diagonally to right, below first stitch and below raw edge, take another small horizontal stitch in same direction. Take a third stitch to right above second stitch on same level as first, and so on. Do not pull thread tight. Rows of horizontal stitches should be between 1/8 and 3/8in (3mm and 1cm) apart.

Oversewing (12). Sometimes known as whipstitch. Has many uses in repairs and renovations and is used for joining two folded edges where strength is needed and for preventing fraying.

Work from right to left, starting with a knot or backstitch. Pass needle at right angles to body through edge. Pull thread through fairly tightly. Repeat to produce a row of neat, slanting stitches. The distance between the stitches varies from 1/16in to 1/8in (2–3mm), depending on thickness of fabric.

Running stitch (13). A weak stitch used for inserting gathering threads or for working French seams by hand on lingerie or children's clothes.

Start with a knot or backstitch and, working from right to left in a straight line, pass needle in and out of fabric at regular intervals. The stitches should be as small as possible and approximately the same size as the spaces between them. If working running stitch for gathering, do not fasten off but leave an end of thread for pulling up gathers when all rows are in place. On a French seam, insert an occasional half or full backstitch for extra strength.

Satin stitch (14). Primarily an embroidery stitch, but useful for strengthening where a full bar tack would be too lumpy, eg. at ends of pockets and buttonholes.

Work in ordinary sewing thread or button thread. Begin with a knot on WS and on RS make parallel small stitches on top of each other or very close together. With thick fabrics, stab needle back and forth from RS to WS. Pull thread tight.

Shell stitch (15). A decorative stitch, equally visible on both sides, and used on fine fabrics to hold a narrow hem or for making tucks.

Work toward you over a prefolded edge, usually about ¼in (6mm) deep. Begin with a small backstitch, make two hemming stitches along the fold, then take needle over and behind folded edge, insert below it and bring through at the same level. Pull thread sufficiently to wrinkle fold attractively. Hold thread with thumb of other hand, take another stitch over fold in same place as first and pull thread tight to hold stitch firmly.

Slipstitch (16). Used for joining two folded edges. It can be invisible if carefully worked, so is useful for anything that has to be sewn from RS, such as a split in a seam or the ends of cuffs and collars.

Start with a knot hidden inside one of the folds. Working from right to left, take a tiny stitch along this fold and then take another in opposite fold about ¹⁄₁₆in (2mm) farther on. Pull thread tight enough to join folds but not to wrinkle them. Fasten off slightly away from join.

Bar tack. A combination of two stitches used for strengthening, eg. at base of zipper opening to prevent fabric tearing. Use ordinary sewing thread.

Start with a knot on WS. With RS toward you, bring needle through to RS and take three or four satin stitches through fabric at point of strain. If there are several layers of fabric to be held, make stitches with a stabbing motion. The length of the stitches will be the length of the bar tack. For full strength, cover these threads with closely spaced blanketstitch, taking needle under strands. Pass needle to WS and fasten off with a backstitch.

HOW TO REMOVE STITCHING

To make any repair or alteration you will have to remove some of the original machine stitching. This need not be tedious, although it must be done carefully to avoid damaging the fabric.

Using a seam ripper.

This can be used in two ways. To remove a few stitches, use the point to lift the loops of each stitch and pull out the thread end. If the stitches to be removed are in the middle of a line or seam, loosen the threads by pushing the point far enough under the first stitch to allow it to be cut by the

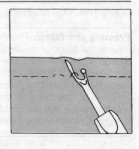

curved blade at the base of the tool.

To open a long seam using the ripper, firmly hold apart the two sides of fabric, stretching the seam between the thumb and forefinger of one hand, and carefully push the cutting blade against the stitch that is visible. Pull the seam open by jerking the two edges apart, cut again with the blade, pull the seam apart again and so on. Note that the blade can easily slip and cut the fabric, especially if it is thin or soft. Avoid this by pushing only until you can hear and feel that the stitch has been cut.

To remove overlocking or other complex machine stitching, lay the blade flat, slide it under the threads and push it along so that it cuts the stitches.

Using your fingers. This is the quickest and easiest way of removing a line of stitching. Loosen the thread at the end of the line, using a pin or the point of the seam ripper, until there is a piece long enough to hold. With the seam to your right, moisten your thumb and forefinger, hold the thread firmly, and tug hard

and sharp to the right (or left if you are left-handed). The thread will have snapped further along the seam. Discard the thread in your hand, turn the seam over and, moistening your fingers, lift up the loose thread left on the surface and jerk it to the right to snap it further along the seam. Repeat the process until you have undone the seam or hem. If the thread fails to break or simply pulls up and wrinkles the fabric, you are not jerking hard enough.

Finally, you could try the method used by experienced dressmakers: remove the stitching by grasping the blades of your small scissors close to the points and snipping and tugging alternately to rip the stitching.

Removing thread ends. Remove odd ends of thread from the fabric using a tweezerbodkin or tweezers or try picking them off or brushing them away with moist fingers.

Pressing the fabric. The thread will have left a row of holes in the fabric which can be removed by pressing with an iron. If the iron alone does not close the holes, use a damp pressing cloth (or wet handkerchief wrung out) and press on that to swell the fibres.

However, depending on the type of alteration or repair you are making, that line of holes may be a useful guideline. It might be more sensible to delay ironing away the holes.

REPAIRS AND REPLACEMENTS

DARNING

Synthetic fibres have reduced the amount of darning in any household, but nevertheless it is a job that still needs doing from time to time. It also happens to be the one that needs the least equipment. Small holes, rips and areas worn thin can be repaired by darning. This is done by weaving a thread or yarn across the hole or over the thin place. Large holes and tears should be patched. See *Patching*, p. 57.

General hints

1. It is easier to darn a thin place before it becomes a hole, so try to catch it sooner rather than later. Keep a check on elbows of sweaters and shirts for signs of wear.

2. You won't want the repair to show too much so try to obtain thread or yarn in the same colour and texture as the article. Ask among family and friends if you can't match it yourself. If you can't find a good match, consider a decorative darn instead.

3. Darning can be done by machine or hand. A few things, such as jeans, work clothes and household linens, may require the more durable machine darn, but hand darning is generally quicker and easier.

4. Keep the darn flat so that it doesn't bubble and don't be depressed by its finished appearance. Pressing with a steam iron or through a damp cloth works wonders.

5. If the garment needs washing, darn it first, otherwise the hole will stretch in the wash.

Darning knitting

Holes. This includes hand and machine knits – anything where you can actually pick up the loops of knitting.

Thread knitting yarn, tapestry wool or darning yarn of a corresponding thickness through a darning or tapestry needle. The needle should be longer than the diameter of the hole. To thread it, wrap the yarn end around the needle to make a flat loop which will pass through the eye (**1**, p. 18). An old-fashioned darning mushroom placed under the hole keeps the garment taut while sewing; an alternative is a child's ball. If you have an embroidery hoop, fix the garment in that. Have the garment RS uppermost. Insert needle ¾in (2cm) from edge of hole. Wiggle point in and out, bringing needle out ¼in (6mm) from hole and keeping a finger on end of yarn to stop it from slipping out of needle. Make

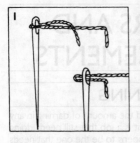

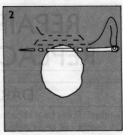

small stitches up to the edge of the hole. Pass needle across hole parallel with the lines of knitting loops in garment, and make stitches on opposite edge of hole for ¼in (6mm) **(2)**.

Pull garment taut to make sure yarn has not reduced size of hole. Turn garment, insert yarn across hole in the same way and repeat until half the hole is filled with strands that touch. The hole is probably round in shape so the outer edge of stitching will be similar. Avoid straight edges and corners as they provide a weak point for further wear. Making small stitches, bring needle into position beside hole, ready to fill second half with strands in the same way **(3)**. Turn garment through 90 degrees and insert second row of yarns. Interlace yarn across hole by weaving needle point over and under alternate strands **(4)**. Keep darn flat. It is worth spending time weaving neatly; the results will be satisfying and impressive. On completion, weave needle at least ¾in (2cm) away from darn and cut off the end of yarn. Also cut off the end of yarn at the start. Press darn lightly on WS using a warm iron over a damp cloth, or a steam iron.

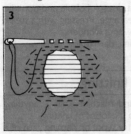

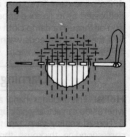

Runs and pulled loops. Knitting snags easily, sometimes breaking loops that will run into ladders. Correct snagging by using the point of a tapestry needle or bodkin and carefully ease the tight yarn back into place until the loop disappears. To repair a run, use a small crochet hook to pick up the loop at the base of the ladder. Pull it up to the next yarn or 'rung' and pull the rung through to form a loop. Lift that loop to the next rung and so on. To prevent further running, use a needle and thread or yarn to sew the loop securely at the top of the ladder.

Thin places. Darn a worn area in a similar manner to a hole but instead of laying down strands, weave the needle over and under the worn lines of knitting. If it is well worn, work in both directions as for a hole but if not, simply cover the area once.

Swiss darn. This is a clever way of reinforcing a thin, worn area on stocking/stockinet stitch. Hold garment RS up, with ribs or wales vertical, and work across the knitting. Thread the yarn through the knitting, taking separate stitches and following precisely the path of the loops of knitting. This is very

easy to do once you have made the first row because you can then loop the new yarn into the line you made.

Darning knit fabric

A thin place or rip in fabric such as track suit jersey can be darned, but a hole should be patched where a darn would be too conspicuous; see *Patching*, p. 57. Follow the instructions above for darning a thin place, using yarn or thread to match the fabric. Work on WS of garment and try not to allow the needle to pass through to RS.

Repair a rip by holding the two torn edges together and join them using a needle and sewing thread with fishbone or lacing stitch. Passing the point first under one raw edge and then the other, angle the needle and space the stitch evenly. For a more durable repair, place a piece of bias fabric or

binding beneath the slit, or even a strip of iron-on interfacing; machine along the rip using running zigzag, serpentine or multi-step stitch to hold the edges together.

Darning woven fabric

Small holes and thin areas may be darned in the same way as knitting. A rip or tear is often the result of an accident, so the edges may be clean-cut. The tear may be straight, but most woven fabrics will tear equally along both warp and weft threads to produce a right-angled tear or hedge tear which can be darned almost invisibly.

By hand. The edges can be held together with fishbone stitch (see previous page), but a more durable repair is the tweed, three-corner, or hedge-tear darn. It is the best repair for coats, skirts, outer wear and good clothes generally. Look on the inside of the garment, on seams and hemline, and try to withdraw some yarns, using a pin. Alternatively, human hair can be used on textured fabrics, tweeds etc. Use sewing thread as a last resort; even a perfect colour match may be visible. Use an ordinary sharps or betweens sewing needle. If the tear is more than ¾in (2cm) long, first hold the torn edges together with fishbone stitch, keeping the fabric RS up. Then work the same darning stitch as described under *Darning knitting*, p. 17, taking the stitches ¼-½in (6-13mm) beyond the edges. Begin at one end and work to the right angle **(1)**. Fasten off the thread. Start again at the far end and overlap the stitching at the angle **(2)**. Press lightly on WS.

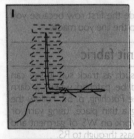
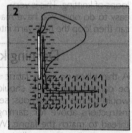

By machine. If you are an experienced sewer and the tear is easy to reach, you may prefer to repair some articles using your sewing machine. Baste a piece of bias binding or press iron-on interfacing to WS of garment, placing it in position with garment RS up and pushing the binding through the slit. Make sure

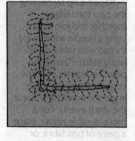

fabric edges are touching before basting or pressing. Select a suitable running zigzag or other wide complex stitch and sew along the tear, going beyond the ends by at least ¼in (6mm). Some modern machines, especially those that are computerized, have a built-in automatic darning facility with a foot and hoop. Older machines may have to be set. Look in the instruction manual for details.

BUTTONHOLES

Fabric buttonholes and those made with thread may become worn, usually because the button is sharp, too big or has rough edges. Repairing them is fiddly, but worthwhile on an otherwise new-looking garment. Iron-on fusible products are a help.

Machine-made buttonholes slightly worn. Trim off ends of thread and fabric on both sides. Draw edges of buttonhole together with a few oversewing stitches. Press flat. Place a piece of paper or tear-away backing underneath and, using your machine, stitch a new buttonhole over the old one. Make it slightly longer and, if possible, use a wider stitch. Ease away the paper and snip any threads between the beads of stitching.

Badly worn. Replace with a different fastening. Remove as much of the old stitching as possible. Draw the edges together and prepare it for machining as above but cover the old buttonhole with a wide satin stitch. Attach an alternative fastening such as Velcro or a snap fastener. Sew the button over the closed buttonhole using a bigger button if you want to cover the stitching completely.

Hand-sewn buttonholes. If only the thread is worn, stitch up the hole and use another fastening as above.

If the buttonhole has pulled away from the garment or if you must retain the fastening, carefully snip and pick out all the remaining thread. Cut a small piece of iron-on interfacing and insert it between the layers of fabric. This type of buttonhole would usually be found on fine fabric so you can probably lift up the facing to do this. If several buttonholes need repairing, use a long strip of interfacing between the layers and re-make the buttonholes using a deeper stitch than previously.

Tailored buttonholes. Made with buttonhole twist over gimp or buttonhole twist, these are found on coats, jackets and outer wear. They are difficult to repair except by a tailor but with care can be converted to another type of buttonhole. Carefully remove all thread, insert a small piece of iron-on interfacing between the layers and press. Convert by following the instructions below for repairing fabric buttonholes, but remember that if you are using this method, all the buttonholes will have to be converted.

Fabric buttonholes. To repair worn fabric buttonholes or convert tailored buttonholes requires care and a degree of sewing skill. You will need a rectangle of new fabric for each, ¾in (2cm) wide, and three times the length of the buttonhole. This could be spare fabric cut from the hem or facing; contrasting fabric or leather, suede etc. Make two pieces of piping for each buttonhole, pressing a strip of Bondaweb/ Wonderunder to WS of the fabric. Peel off the paper backing, fold strip WS inside, with raw edges even, and press to make strips ⅜in (1cm) wide **(1)**.

Remove old buttonholes. Begin by snipping stitching on WS of garment to detach facing. If garment is lined you will have to undo stitching holding lining to facing. Undo remainder of buttonhole and remove the pieces of fabric. Remove all thread ends. Press fabric flat using tip of iron to ease out edges that are folded under. Cut a strip of iron-on interfacing 1½in (4cm) wide and place it adhesive side up under the outer layer of garment. Push raw edges of fabric together. Press well.

On outside, holding garment facing clear, place prepared pipings in pairs with cut edges directly over position of previous buttonhole. Baste pipings in position or secure with pieces of basting tape. Using tailor's chalk or fabric marking pen, draw a line across pipings to indicate size of buttonhole, making it at least ⅛in (3mm) longer at each end than the old one **(2)**. Stitch pipings to garment as follows: starting in the middle, machine or hand backstitch along centre of piping as far as mark; turn, stitch to mark at far end, turn and stitch back to the middle **(3)**. Repeat on all pipings.

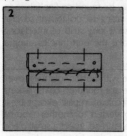

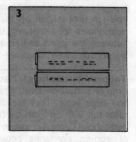

Check for accuracy – on WS you should see two parallel lines of stitching. Cut the interfacing between the rows of stitching to within ¼in (6mm) of each end and cut at an angle to the end of each line **(4)**. Do not cut piping strips. Push pipings through slit to WS, flatten with fingers. Baste together with thread or basting tape to hold folded edges of piping together. At each end of buttonhole, tuck the triangle of fabric out of sight. Press buttonhole on both sides. Stitch around buttonhole along the seamline between pipings and garment, with a machine or by hand, stitching back and forth with a stabbing movement **(5)**. Pipings in leather can be kept flat using a small amount of adhesive.

Replace garment facing, baste facing to garment, stitching

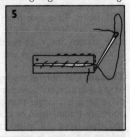

round each buttonhole (except leather). Turn under edges of facing around each buttonhole and sew firmly with hemming **(6)**, or secure with basting, and then work another row of machine stitching from RS of garment. You may need to lengthen the slit in the facing to fit a larger buttonhole.

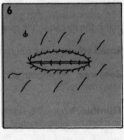

Snip basting between edges of piping. Press to finish.

Buttonholes not up to standard. If you have worked a line of buttonholes that are not very good or wrongly spaced, cover them up! Using a folded strip of fabric, topstitch it to the outside of the garment leaving the outer edge free, so making a concealed or fly fastening.

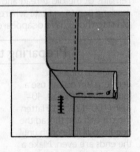

BUTTONS

The proud boast of reluctant sewers is that they can't sew on a button – just like cooks who can't boil an egg. Surely no-one can get through life without EVER sewing on a button! It requires no previous experience, and demonstrates the truth of the old proverb, a stitch in time saves nine – what could be more infuriating than a lost button?

Equipment

Half the battle is to have the necessary equipment handy. You will need:

Needle. Size 4, 5 or 6 sharps or betweens needle; a small thin needle (6) for thin fabric; larger thicker needle (4) for thick fabric. Take one from the middle of your assorted needle pack and that will be near enough. Check that you have chosen the right needle by pushing it through the fabric: if this is hard work use a smaller size.

Thread. Use normal sewing thread for light and medium weight fabric: spun polyester or core-spun/cotton-wrapped polyester are stronger than cotton threads. Use heavy duty polyester thread, linen or button thread for leather, canvas and coat fabrics. If in doubt have a look at the thread holding the other buttons in place. Keep a supply of the basic colours: black, white, grey, brown and navy thread plus other shades that go with your wardrobe. If you can't match the thread to the garment, match it to the button.

Small scissors. For cutting the thread.

Beeswax. To smooth and strengthen thread. See *Sewing Equipment*, p. 6.

Thimble. You will certainly need one for sewing buttons on tough canvas or leather.

You might need a pin or seam ripper to help remove the remains of the old thread and you might also need a fabric marking pen to indicate where to position the button if the old stitch holes have disappeared.

Preparing the thread

See *How to thread a needle*, p.9. You can use a long piece of thread, 40–48in (100–120cm). Flatten the cut end and thread the needle; pull it through until the ends are even. Make a knot. Hold thread by the knot and run it firmly over the cake of beeswax as far as the needle. Repeat twice. With knot held between 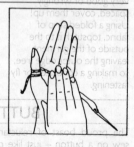 thumb and forefinger of left (or right) hand and thread hanging down across your hand, rub the palm of right hand firmly across left from finger tips to wrist. You will see that the threads have twisted into a rope. Wind twisted section around left thumb to leave next section hanging across palm. Continue to twist and wind until you reach the needle. Gently pull thread from thumb without untwisting. The wax will keep the strands together and also provide a coating which lubricates and prolongs the life of the thread. This button needle will be sufficient for three small or two large buttons. If you have more than that to sew on, prepare extra needles before you begin. If there is a half length or more left when you have finished, knot the end and put the needle away ready for next time.

How to sew on a button

Follow this method and the button could stay in place forever! If the garment is torn or you are using heavy fabric or a particular type of button, consult the sections which follow, pp. 26-7.

1. Pick out all traces of thread from garment.
2. Hold garment RS uppermost. Insert needle through old stitch marks, piercing through to underside. Pass needle back to upperside. Make another stitch the same **(1)**. Cut off the knot on the surface of the fabric. Make a third stitch.
3. Slip button onto needle, insert needle through opposite hole straight into garment and out again beneath the button **(2)**. To do this the button will be standing on edge. Make six more stitches in this way.

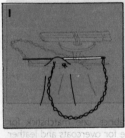
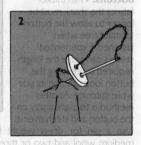

4. If the button has four holes, make three stitches across the first pair of holes, then three more across the other pair of holes.
5. Bring needle out beneath button. Due to the position of the button during sewing there is a space between button and garment, which forms a shank to keep button clear of the garment. Wind thread tightly round shank four or five times **(3)**. Take three stitches across base of shank to hold button steady.
6. Pass needle to underside where you will find several threads. Take a few stitches over these threads **(4)**. If you know how to do blanketstitch it will finish the threads off neatly. Take two more stitches through the threads and snip off remaining button thread.

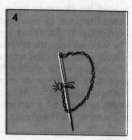

The method described is suitable for attaching buttons to all lightweight fabrics. Thicker fabrics require longer shanks.

Lost buttons. If there is no spare button attached to the garment find one similar in size, thickness, colour and style. If it is not a good match put the odd one where it will least show (for example, hidden under a tie or on the tuck-in) and put the good one in its place. Alternatively, sew two new buttons to cuffs and put the cuff buttons on the front. You can replace the whole lot with new ones, which is a good idea if several have broken or if sharp edges have worn the threads.

Jacket, coat and dress buttons.

With thicker fabrics the shank must be longer to allow the button to stand free when fastened. Experienced sewers can judge the length required by keeping the button loose and on its side while stitching. Another method is to place a stay on the button and stitch over it.

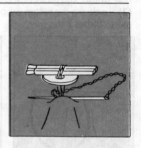

Use a pin for dress weight fabrics, one matchstick for medium wool and two or three for overcoats and leather clothes. Remove the stay before winding thread around shank.

Dome/shank buttons.

These have metal loops on the back which act as a shank, but to prevent the button wobbling you should still wind thread round three or four times.

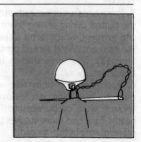

Backing buttons. Thick or heavy garments or those made from soft fabric should have a backing button on their underside. These are small flat buttons with two large holes. They will keep the garment flat and prevent wear and distortion of the fabric. Attach the main button through two holes (or three

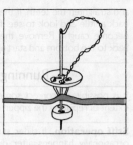

stitches if two-hole) allowing for a long shank. Put backing button in place and complete the stitching by stabbing the needle back and forth through both sets of holes. Keep the shank on the main button; the backing button should lie flat on the fabric.

False fastening buttons. These are for decoration and should be attached flat without a shank.

Bored buttons. In duffle coat toggles and some wooden and moulded plastic buttons the hole is tunnelled through the button. You must make a thread shank or the button will undo in wear.

Attaching by machine. Most modern machines can be used to sew buttons; some have a stitch setting especially for that purpose. In all two-hole buttons the holes are the same distance apart. Follow the instructions in your sewing machine manual.

Torn garment. Buttons often come off because the fabric beneath them tears. Remove all old thread ends. Mark button position using fabric marking pen, then press garment to flatten torn edges. Using point of bodkin or head of a pin, gently push a small piece of Wundaweb/Stitch Witchery through the tear so that it lies between the layers of fabric. Smooth it out, replace torn edges to cover it and press, placing a damp cloth on top. If both layers of fabric are torn, or if you don't feel the webbing is sufficient reinforcement, fold a small piece of seam binding or tape and place it on the underside of the garment, stitching through it when attaching the button.

ZIPPERS

Manufacturers often use six lines of stitching or more to put in a zipper, so it frequently happens that it is the zipper that breaks rather than the stitching. A broken zipper is generally the result of too tight a fit, too short an opening or rough use. You can avoid breakages by remembering to fasten the waistband before the zipper. Flatten the garment and straighten the teeth. If the slider sticks, stop and ease it back a little and look to see if a facing, lining or thread has become caught. Remove the obstruction, take the slider back to the bottom and start again.

Running repairs

It is possible to correct some faults without going to the extent of replacing the zipper.

Stiff operation. If slider sticks or is hard to pull, which occasionally happens after dry-cleaning, you can ease it. Return slider to bottom. If zipper has metal teeth, run a lead pencil over them along the edges; use beeswax along polyester or nylon teeth.

Jams. If slider sticks at one point, move it back and examine the teeth. Sometimes a tooth moves slightly out of alignment and you can easily move it back. Occasionally you may find one tooth has become damaged; this can be rubbed smooth with an emery board or nail file.

If lining or fly facing has become caught, fold it back flat and gently ease slider back to bottom. If jam is severe and fabric too thick to do this, snip fabric in front of slider and move it slowly forward.

Broken tab. If the tab breaks off the slider, replace it with a key ring, or thread a short piece of cord or tape through the hole in the slider.

Broken stitching. At the first sign of stitching giving way, replace it. Using a pin, release a little more thread on each side of breakage. Pull through both ends of thread and tie in a knot. Pull edge of tape back into position and hem it to the seam allowance. Replace the gap with two rows of hand backstitch or machin-ing, overlapping ends of original stitching by at least ¾in (2cm).

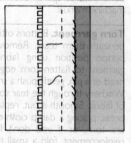

Broken tooth. If one tooth of a metal zipper moves or breaks away from the tape, the slider will jam below it. This usually happens near the bottom of the zipper and it can be repaired. Snip edge of tape below the troublesome tooth **(1)**, carefully lift it and gently move slider up so that it locks the two lines of teeth together. Take slider to top. Using double thread, work a strong bar tack of at least eight stitches across the teeth just above the repaired tooth **(2)**.

This will prevent slider from going to the bottom again. In an emergency a safety pin or an office staple can be used until you can stitch the bar tack.

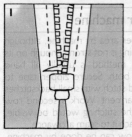

Teeth out of line. It frequently happens below the waistband of trousers that one side of the zipper has become curved in wear, and does not quite meet the opposite side. Remove stitching holding zipper tape to trousers. Press fabric and tape with a damp cloth. Baste zipper to fabric, slightly further in than previously. Stitch twice firmly, overlapping ends of original stitching by at least ¾in (2cm).

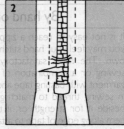

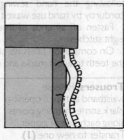

Replacing a zipper

If all else fails buy a new zipper. The following guidelines will help you set it in correctly.

1. Measure the length of the toothed part and buy a new zipper the same length. If you buy a special trouser zipper it may be too long, so set it into the opening beginning at the bottom, tucking the surplus into the waistband and cutting it off if necessary.

2. Use fabric marking pen or tailor's chalk and make strokes across tape of old zipper and garment before removing stitching. Transfer marks to new zipper. You can then be sure you've got the new one in the right place.

3. Use small scissors or a seam ripper.

4. Open and close slider between each process just to make sure all is well.

5. Look at the way the zipper had been put in; the last row of stitching inserted will be the first for you to remove. You will also have to remove part of the waist or neckline finish, or some lining stitching.

6. On skirts and trousers, working on one side at a time will ensure that you don't lose your way. Use basting tape, placed on RS of zipper tapes, to secure zipper for stitching. Thread basting does not hold zipper steady.

7. If possible follow the old stitching marks.

By hand or machine?

It is not easy to reach a zipper area by machine, although you may feel your hand stitching is not strong enough on its own. The most satisfactory method is usually all hand sewing or a combination of both. Secure zipper tape to garment with basting tape and stitch with small backstitches in sewing thread to match garment. Work a second row beside it for strength or, if the stitching would be visible, hem along edge of tape to attach it to seam allowance.

Alternatively, the second row can be done by machine, following the hand sewing. When stitching denim or corduroy by hand use waxed double thread.

Fasten off all ends of thread very strongly with six or eight stitches.

On completion press RS, sliding the tip of the iron beside the teeth to avoid marks and damage to the iron.

Trousers. Release waistband at top of opening. Mark some matching points along each side of zipper. Transfer to new one **(1)**. Remove bar tack at base of zipper, ie. right side on men's trousers, left side on women's skirts and trousers, and remove that side of zipper. Press edge of garment taking care not to stretch it.

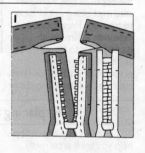

Place new zipper in position, matching marks, and secure with basting tape **(2)**. Stitch through zipper tape, seam allowance and garment. If there is a fly facing, replace it and stitch again. Next undo second side of old zipper, press edge and baste in new zipper. Match up marks and close slider to make sure it is in correct position. Open slider and stitch. Work a strong bar tack at base of opening **(3)**.

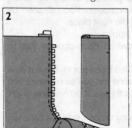

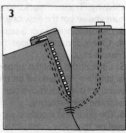

Dress. Release collar, facing, lining or whatever, from top of opening. Insert several marks between tape and dress along each side of zipper. Transfer marks to new zipper. From the outside oversew edges of dress together with basting stitches. Remove old zipper and place new one in position RS down over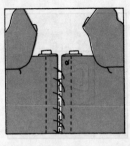

seam. Secure with basting tape. Stitch along each side with dress RS up, following original stitching line. Replace the trimmings and work a bar tack on RS at base of opening. Press lightly beside zipper teeth.

FASTENINGS

Fastenings usually fail because the stitching is not strong or secure enough. Sometimes a fastening itself breaks, but this is likely to be because it was unequal to the strain put on it. If you find a particular fastener habitually needs repairing or replacing, read the section of this book devoted to *Adjustments for Fit and Comfort*, pp. 89-111. It could be that an alteration would be the answer. Sometimes fastenings on bought clothes are too fiddly – often things like hooks are very small. So if they come off, take the opportunity to improve on the size, or even switch to a different type of fastener, to prolong the life of the garment. If the material is damaged, repair it with a piece of fabric, seam binding, tape or iron-on material before attaching the new fastener.

Hooks and eyes

It will nearly always be an improvement to replace an old hook and eye with a larger one. If one part has come off it is likely that it will not be long before the other part joins it so re-stitch both halves. Do not remove both parts together, or you may lose the position. Carefully remove any thread holding the eye or bar. If fabric is torn, hem a piece of seam binding or tape over worn area. Fasten old hook into new eye or bar, find the correct position and pin down the eye. Release hook **(I)**. Start with a knot, then bring needle up in one loop of the eye. Take one stitch over the loop; put needle into fabric and bring it up in the other loop. Remove the pin.

There is no better way of attaching than with buttonhole stitch. Hooks and eyes, properly sewn, will stay put for ever, so take the trouble to learn how to do it. The stitch is worked coming toward you. Insert the needle with the point emerging inside one loop. Grasp the thread close to the eye of the needle and wind it around the point of the

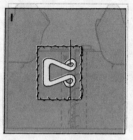
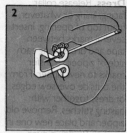

needle, first away, then toward you, under the point. Push on the needle and withdraw it. As you do this a little knot forms which moves down onto the surface of the fabric as you pull the needle. Help the knot by taking hold of the thread and gently easing it down. Make the next stitch and settle the knot so that it touches the first **(2)**. Continue in this way until the eye is covered with close neat stitches. Pass needle under fabric to second part and stitch in the same way **(3)**. Fasten off thread.

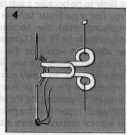

Remove old hook, fasten new one into new eye, locate correct position and pin hook to garment. Unfasten hook. Sew the head first, taking six or seven deep stitches under the part that curls over **(4)**. Pass needle through fabric and work buttonhole stitch around each loop, as for the eye.

If the original fastening wobbled in wear, attach a metal bar or make a thread one. Mark the exact position where the head of the hook will come then make a bar of four threads the width of the hook, but place them ¹⁄₁₆in (2mm) beyond the marked position to allow for the give that will occur. Work blanketstitch closely over the threads. Fasten off securely.

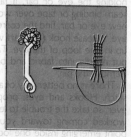

Hook in seam. Only the head should project from the seamed edge of the garment. Undo some of the seam stitching, remove the hook completely and re-stitch it, or put in a replacement in the same position. Stitch very securely, waxing the thread for strength, as this type of fastening is normally used on heavy or thick fabric.

Bra and corset hooks. These are usually close together and set into a seam with a protective extension. It is often the seam stitching that gives way. Examine the construction of the garment and if you can stitch it by machine then do so, but if it would run the risk of breaking the needle, backstitch strongly by hand. If the edging has worn or if hooks are broken, remove the entire section and replace with a bra back replacement kit (see p. 43). Cut the strip to length and finish each end with oversewing. Place the strip under the edge of the garment and machine or backstitch twice for strength.

Trouser hooks. These are made from flat metal and they fasten into flat bars. Re-stitch using double, waxed button thread and buttonhole stitch. If the hook was originally concealed, with only the head extending, undo the waistband stitching nearby and lift off the facing. Re-stitch the hook and replace the waistband by slipstitching around the edge.

A stronger attachment can be made using cotton tape or stay tape. Loop the tape through the hook as shown and hem around the ends, stitching firmly into the waistband.

A concealed trouser bar can be repaired in the same way, either with buttonhole stitch or using seam binding or tape.

Snap fasteners

These are not strong so you may want to take the opportunity of replacing with a hook and eye or a larger snap for extra strength. Sometimes a sharp edge cuts through the thread so check the snap before sewing the same one back on. If it is hanging on by a few stitches remove the whole thing and all thread ends. If both halves of snap need re-stitching, replace one piece at a time or you may lose the position. If the fabric is damaged, darn the area before replacing the snap. If there is a hole in the fabric, cover it by hemming around a small piece of seam binding or tape, or insert a piece of iron-on interfacing or fusible web into the hole; smooth over the fibres and press.

The knob section of a snap goes on the outer part of the opening; the well or socket part is sewn underneath facing outward. Attach the knob first. Place snap in position, insert a pin through central hole and pierce fabric beneath **(1)**. Take first stitch under snap to conceal knot and bring needle up through one of the holes. Take needle over the edge and bring it up through a hole on the opposite side.

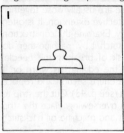
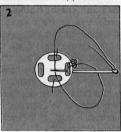

The snap is now anchored. Remove pin. Take needle underneath again and bring it up through another hole. Work buttonhole stitch **(2)** as described under *Hooks and eyes*, p. 31. The stitches must be close and the knots touching. Each hole will require four to six stitches, depending on the size of the snap. The stitches should not penetrate all layers of fabric. Fasten off securely beside the snap.

Attach the socket section of the snap: with edges of garment correctly in position, insert a pin from the outside of garment through hole in knob section, and a layer of garment beneath. Insert needle and take a stitch where the pin pierces the lower layer of garment **(3)**. Remove pin. Place socket section of snap in position over stitch, anchor it by stitching through two holes and attach with buttonhole stitch as previously described.

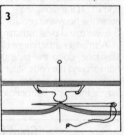

Snaps on tape. These can be bought in lengths and offer a useful alternative to a row of conventional snaps, especially on household items, sports and children's clothes. Attach the knob section to the outer layer with the sockets facing outward. Mark position on garment using fabric marking pen.

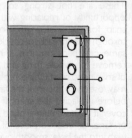

Measure required amount of tape and cut between snaps, allowing at least ⅜in (1cm) on either side. Separate the pieces and attach knob section first. Fold under one end of the tape, place in position and pin at intervals between snaps. Fold under second end. Place the two edges of garment together, one on top of the other, and pin socket section of tape in position, adjusting it so that corresponding halves of snap are even. Hem by hand all around each piece of tape or if you prefer to stitch by machine, attach the one-sided zipper or piping foot in order to stitch beside the snaps. Some of the latest machines have a different design of zipper foot that cannot be used for this which means you will have to hand stitch.

Plastic snaps. These are square and come in white, pink, blue or transparent. They are less bulky than metal ones and although not strong, are very useful on baby clothes and where a single fastener is needed. Attach as for snaps, making three buttonhole stitches in each corner.

Snap fasteners with decorative caps. Because of the way in which these caps and rings are clamped to the fabric you may find it difficult to replace them. Remove all parts, using pliers if necessary. Repair the fabric with a patch (see *Patching*, p. 57) or iron-on interfacing. Attach new fasteners using a larger size if possible. Alternatively, use a different form of fastening such as Velcro.

Jeans snaps. These are clamped to the fabric so firmly that when they come off they usually take a piece of fabric with them. If the snap itself does break, remove all remaining parts. Repair the fabric by inserting iron-on interfacing into the hole and also apply a denim patch to the area. As an acceptable alternative, clamp a jeans button to the under-side and make a buttonhole in the upper layer; see *Buttonholes*, p. 20.

Fabric or rouleau tubing loops

These do not generally come off but the fastening may wobble after persistent use. Either tighten the loop by working a bar tack at the base or replace the buttons with larger ones.

Frogs and toggles

The stitching may give way or the garment may strain this insecure fastening. To tighten the fastening, cover the ends of the frogs and part of the loop with triangles of fabric or leather. Stabilize toggles by winding double waxed thread several times between button and garment. If the fastening is unsatisfactory, remove the frogs and toggles and replace with buttons and buttonholes or Velcro fasteners.

Velcro tape

This is a useful fastener for waistbands, cuffs and so on but becomes less effective if fluff is allowed to collect under the hooks. Keep it clean with a teazle brush. Cheaper types of press fastener may wear out with use. Replace with Velcro tape, which is easily re-stitched when necessary. Always use enough for a firm fastening: at least 1 1/4in (3cm) at waists and where there is moving pressure on the garment; 5/8in (1.5cm) is enough on cuffs or to hold an edge, possibly instead of using a snap fastener. On an opening longer than about 2in (5cm) use a continuous piece of the loop side but space out short pieces of the hook side to keep the opening flexible. Since the greatest strain is at the opening, you can strengthen

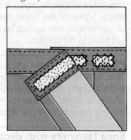

the stitching by rounding the corners of the Velcro tape. It also helps if the hook side is 1/16in (2mm) shorter than the loop side. Sew the tape by hand with small hemming stitches. If you find it tough, change to a smaller needle. To stitch by machine, sew over the edge with a small zigzag. With both methods, start in the middle, not at a corner, and overlap the stitching by at least 3/8in (1cm).

Spot-ons/Velcoin fasteners. These are discs of Velcro fastener with self-adhesive backs which can be used singly or in series to replace almost any kind of fastening. The soft side should normally face the body. The adhesive holds them in place while you hem around the edge, or machine stitch a triangle or square across the middle of each disc.

ELASTIC

Elastic has to be sufficiently tight to grip, and the constant strain usually makes it wear out long before the garment itself. Also, as it is most often used in lightweight clothing and undergarments, constant washing tends to make it deteriorate. Replacing it is not difficult – but unless you keep a stock of several types, emergency replacements may have to be made with a different type from that originally found in the garment.

Types

Baby elastic is narrow with a flat soft rubber centre.
Ribbed elastic made in many widths, is stronger and has several yarn-coated cores of rubber running through it.
Open weave elastic, sometimes wrongly named 'shirring

elastic', is a polyurethane and rubber mesh, also made in various widths. It is light and cool to wear. **Single core** elastic is round and springy and difficult to join. **Shirring** elastic, also known as elastic sewing thread, is a fine single core, covered with white or coloured yarn. Since its function is decorative, it is not strong and can only be stitched in place, not threaded. There is also a variety of elastics for special purposes, such as decorative edging for underwear and strong, fluted elastic for men's underwear.

Replacing

Use a width similar to or narrower than the original. Feel for the join and see if it has been stitched into a seam before removing stitching. Take out the old elastic and press the garment before inserting the replacement. A shorter piece will usually be needed unless the old one snapped because it was too tight.

Use an elastic threader, tweezerbodkin or rouleau needle/ball end bodkin to thread elastic through casing. A safety-pin can also be used; it is easy to attach to the elastic but more difficult to handle inside the casing. If a gap has been made in the stitching, it should be equal to the width of the elastic.

Measuring

The length of elastic to use depends on its width and the part of the body it will be fitting. Fleshy parts such as the waist can stand a tighter grip than bony areas such as wrists and ankles. Elastic around the upper arm is difficult to fit, as the sleeve moves over the muscle area. Elastic on nightwear, sports clothes and children's clothes should not be too tight.

Measure elastic around the body, add 1 in (2.5cm) for the join and 1½in (4cm) for ease if the fabric is bulky.

Joining ends of elastic

The efficiency of the elastic depends upon the strength of the join.

Flat join. Overlap ends by at least ⅜in (1cm), more for wide elastic, oversew along sides and blanketstitch or buttonhole stitch by hand along raw edges (1). To stitch by machine, use a wide zigzag and sew across elastic twice, covering raw edges (2).

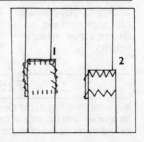

Sports join. Hold ends with raw edges together and machine across twice at least ⅝in (1.5cm) from end.

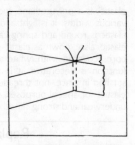

Adjustable safety join. Useful on children's and exercise clothes. Hold ends with raw edges together and machine across 1in (2.5cm) from end and again ⅜in (1cm) from end. If it proves too tight undo the inner join.

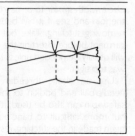

Seam join. With ends of elastic extending from casing, anchor with a pin. With seam edges even, stitch from garment through casing and fasten stitching securely. Stitch again through casing for strength. Trim ends neatly.

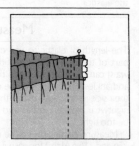

Flattening a lumpy join. You may have zigzagged or overlocked the seam which tends to make it stand away, causing a lump. Flatten seam after stitching by folding towards back of garment and stitching from RS a small rectangle:

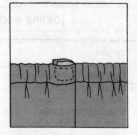

Fitting

It may be necessary to put the garment on, or even wear it for a while, with the ends of the elastic pinned together, before trimming and joining to fit comfortably.

Making replacements

Casing or hem. Feel for join in elastic, remove enough stitching at that point to enable you to pull elastic out. Cut elastic to withdraw. If any part is unworn cut it off and keep it for future use. Cut a new piece of elastic, thread it or sew it to the end of a bodkin and thread it through the casing. Pull both

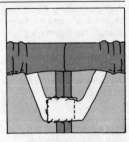

ends clear and join. Replace stitching in casing. Depending on the garment, you may wish to do this by machine to match original stitching, but if the appearance is not important it is much easier to work hemming or slipstitch across the gap.

Wide casing or hem. Wide elastic inserted in a casing or hem tends to wear out, especially at points of strain, because it has to be worn tight. Locate join in elastic, cut stitching and remove it. The same width elastic may be inserted, as described previously, but a more comfortable, longer-lasting repair can be made. This is particularly useful on sports clothes, because if one piece gives way all is not lost.

Use two lengths of narrow elastic that will fit side by side in the casing and allow ⅜in (1cm) ease. Mark along the centre of casing using a fabric marking pen. Make two slots in a seam, each wide enough to take the elastic. This may involve opening part of the seam and even the stitching along the casing edge. Re-stitch seam, leaving the theading slots and firmly fastening thread ends **(1)**. Press seam edges open. Fold casing back into position and press. If seam is difficult to reach, slots may be made by removing a few stitches with a seam ripper. Stop seam from coming undone further by working bar tacks by hand at the ends of the slots. Machine stitch along marked line on casing and replace any broken stitching at lower edge **(2)**. Insert each piece of elastic, trim to size and join.

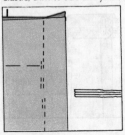

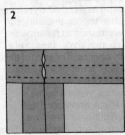

Hand stitching. The methods that follow utilize machine stitching. If you haven't access to a machine, stitch by hand, hemming over the edge of the elastic and then working back over it the other way with oversewing to form a strong cross stitch.

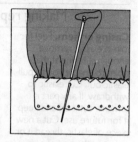

Flat edge. Pyjama and track suit trouser waists often have the elastic attached flat inside the trousers, usually with several rows of stitching. When it needs replacing there is nothing for it but to remove all rows of stitching, press the garment and attach a new piece of soft elastic. Divide elastic

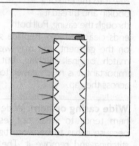

and garment into four with a fabric marking pen, match corresponding points and pin. Stitch with elastic uppermost, stretching it as you stitch. Use a zigzag stitch and begin with the line of stitching nearest the upper edge.

If the trousers can stand shortening, cut off the old elastic to save having to remove stitching. Make a new hem by pressing a 1/4in (6mm) fold of fabric onto WS. Apply elastic as described above.

Narrow casing or hem. If the casing or hem is very narrow, as it sometimes is on quilted clothes, swimwear and household goods, it may mean that the elastic is stitched to the fabric inside the casing. It cannot simply be withdrawn when worn out; you will have to undo the casing as well as the elastic. Make and stitch a new casing slightly deeper than the original. Insert elastic as for *Casing* (see previous page).

Fly opening. Shorts, pyjamas and children's clothes often feature an elasticized waistband that fastens with a button across the top of a fly opening. The ends of the elastic are anchored in the ends of the waistband which means it will be difficult to replace it. Cut off button and remove thread ends. Remove sufficient

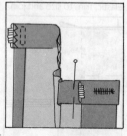

stitching to release the elastic and pull it to loosen it inside the waistband. If you can, pull it until the other end is in sight, then cut through the elastic, close to the stitching, possibly beside the buttonhole. The alternative is to try to remove the stitching holding the other end. Press the garment. To replace with new elastic, on the inside of the waistband, near the buttonhole, cut a vertical slit. Insert elastic. Pin the end to the waistband where it emerges from the slit. Machine or backstitch across waistband through all layers. Remove pin, tuck end of elastic inside band and make a rectangle of stitching to close slit and anchor elastic. At the far end of the waistband, pull the end of the elastic out, adjust to size, and pin. Stitch across waistband through all layers. Trim end of elastic so that it is level with the band and make a rectangle of stitching to hold elastic and close the end of the band.

Thread casing.
Knitted skirts and trousers sometimes have the elastic attached flat to the knitting to minimize bulk. It is difficult to replace it by the above method, as the knitting tends to stretch. Remove old elastic, taking care not to snip the knitting. Cut new elastic to length and join the ends. With skirt

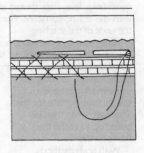

WS out, slip elastic over it. Using knitting yarn in a tapestry or knitters' needle, make a casing for the elastic by working herringbone stitch across it. Work from left to right taking stitches alternately above and below the edge of the elastic. On completion tie ends of yarn together then darn them into the skirt.

Open weave elastic.
This type of elastic wears out quickly. It is usually attached to the garment with two or more rows of stitching. Remove all stitching to remove elastic. Press the garment. Cut and join elastic to fit. Divide elastic and garment into four, mark with fabric pen. With garment RS

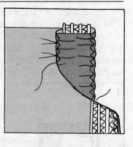

uppermost, overlap elastic by ¼in (6mm). Match the quarters and stitch within edge of elastic using zigzag or stretch stitch. Fold elastic completely to inside of garment and stitch again inside lower and upper edges, stretching elastic to its maximum.

Shirring elastic. This is usually found in blocks of several rows and it can become slack in wear, but its life can be prolonged by holding it in the steam from a kettle.

If this treatment has no effect, undo the whole lot, taking care not to damage the fabric, which can be revived by washing and pressing to close up the stitch holes. To replace shirring, wind single core shirring elastic onto a machine bobbin. Use the machine mechanism in order to wind it under tension; doing it by hand is seldom successful as the elastic slackens. Put polyester thread on top of the machine and set a large straight or zigzag stitch. Stitch straight lines with fabric RS up. After the first row you will need to keep the fabric flat and use the edge of the foot as a guide to keep lines parallel. Depending on the fabric, it will be three of four rows before any ruching occurs. If the area is continuous, a wrist for example, stitch round and round in a continuous line. Pass thread ends to WS and tie together with the elastic to fasten. For extra strength zigzag across the ends of the stitching.

Alternatively, if the fabric seems worn after removing the stitching, apply the elastic flat to WS, couching it down with a zigzag stitch set wide enough to straddle elastic.

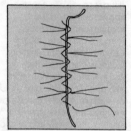

Stretch elastic as you stitch; some machines have a special foot or plate for this. The elastic may then be pulled up to ruche the fabric further.

With both methods, finish by holding the garment in the steam from a kettle to release the tension in the elastic.

Stretched ribbing. Knitted welts and cuffs often slacken in wear. If the ribbing is folded double, carefully snip the stitches at the seam and insert a length of wide elastic. Make a flat join and re-stitch the ribbing **(1)**.

Single ribbing can be tightened by using special transparent knit-in elastic. Use a large darning needle and weave the elastic in and out of the ribs on WS **(2)**. Work round and round and fasten ends securely.

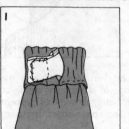

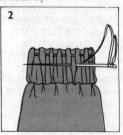

Bra fastenings. Remove stitching at the point where the elastic joins the bra fabric. This will also remove the worn fastening. Use a commercially available bra back replacement kit, trimming the ends of the elastic to size if necessary. Overlap bra onto new elastic and stitch several times back and forth with a zigzag stitch.

Bra straps. Replacement kits are available or you can use soft, brushed elastic of a suitable width – this is a chance to change to a wider, more comfortable strap – and measure the length carefully against existing straps. Undo stitching to remove old straps. Overlap bra onto elastic and stitch across it at least twice. If the original elastic was covered with a bias strip, either cut it off or place the new elastic on top.

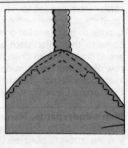

Suspender/garter belts.
Remove stitching to remove old suspenders/garters. Using a suspender/garter repair kit attach new suspenders/garters using zigzag or stretch stitch. If the elastic with the kit is not long enough, replace it with longer pieces, stitching firmly to the suspenders/garters before attaching them to the belt. If the waist elastic wears out, slit the fabric on WS to remove it and insert a new piece, stitching across each end at least twice for strength.

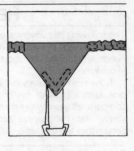

Elastic edging. Elastic is often attached to the edges of underwear. It eliminates the bulk of a hem and is a quick manufacturing method. The elastic is usually soft and sometimes decorative, so it tends to wear out quickly. Sometimes it pulls off the garment edge, more usually it loses its elasticity. Locate the seam in which ends of elastic are stitched and undo it to a point 1in (2.5cm) below edge of elastic. Remove elastic from garment taking care not to damage the fabric. This will

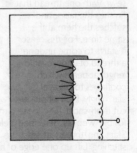

be a tedious job especially if the stitching also finishes the edge of the garment. Press the garment. Cut new elastic of a similar type to original to fit the body and mark into four equal sections using a fabric marking pen. Also mark edge of garment into four on RS. Matching quarters, overlap edge of elastic onto garment and pin at seam edges and marks. Set your machine on zigzag, triple zigzag, stretch or any stitch recommended for stitching elastic. With garment RS up, stitch along lower edge of elastic. Stretch elastic in each quarter so that it lies flat on the fabric. Remove pins as you come to them. Backstitch at each end to fasten off. For added strength or to finish raw edge of garment, a second row of stitching can be made beside the first. With garment inside out and ends of elastic together, re-stitch seam; stitch twice across elastic for strength.

Men's underpants. The original elastic may have a fluted non-elastic edging stitched flat to the top of the garment. If you are unable to purchase the same type use conventional soft elastic and replace as described above.

HEMS

The following instructions are for making running repairs to skirts, trousers, sleeves or whatever. If the entire garment needs lengthening or shortening, read *Renovations and Improvements*, p. 71.

If the repair involves cutting the garment, mark it with pins, tailor's chalk or marking pen before cutting. Always compare left seam with right seam, left leg with right leg, left sleeve with right sleeve and so on to make absolutely certain they are the same.

Re-stitching a short length. Hems of shop-bought clothes are usually sewn with one thread that finishes the fabric and stitches the hem at the same time. For this reason, if it starts to come undone a thread of unbelievable length appears which continues to unravel alarmingly. Do not pull it:

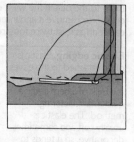

cut it off short. The loose part of the hem can be held with fusible web as described below, or it can be hand sewn. Start the thread at least 1in (2.5cm) from end of original stitching. Lift up one edge of hem and make a stitch to link it to garment. Hem with catch stitch – which is worked from right to left – picking up a very small amount of fabric each time on the needle and leaving gaps in between of ¼in

(6mm). If more than half of original stitching has come undone, pull out the remainder and re-stitch entire hem. Press WS lightly.

Fused hem. Use in an emergency and as a permanent hem on medium-weight fabrics. The turn-up of the fabric must be 1/16in (2mm) wider than the fusible web you use. Even up hem edge and oversew if it frays. Alternatively, zigzag the edge or cut with pinking shears. Fold up hem onto

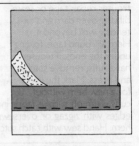

WS and press. Soft fabrics, skirts and dresses will need basting first. Keep stitching close to fold. Arrange hem on pressing surface and put fusible web under the edge, making sure it is completely covered by hem. It may be easier to do this in short lengths. Using a hot iron over a damp cloth, press hem with firm sharp movements. Continue all round hem. Remove any basting stitches and press hem again, this time from RS.

Remember that a stronger hemming web is available for use on denim.

Jeans hem. Badly frayed hems will have to be cut off. If it is the edge that is worn, remove all stitching, press flat, then trim off worn part, cutting both legs equally and straight. Make a new hem by folding raw edge twice. Baste and press. Machine all round near edge, or hem by hand. If trousers are only slightly

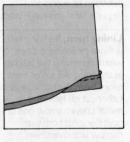

worn, undo worn area and press a piece of soft iron-on interfacing onto WS. Replace hem and re-stitch.

Jersey hem. Jersey is likely to become uneven and the thread worn. Remove all stitching and press fabric, trimming edge if uneven. Fold up edge, baste and press lightly to avoid stretching. With RS up stitch around hem twice, once close to the bottom and again below the raw edge. More stitching may be added in between.

Frayed trousers. Undo hem and repair torn area with a hand darn. Re-stitch hem. Place a length of trouser repair tape or seam binding over darn and extending well beyond it. Hem all round tape, folding under the ends. If trousers have cuffs, remove stitching and press. Mark the length for a new hem without cuffs. Trim off surplus fabric including worn area. Finish raw edges with zigzag or oversewing. Fold up, baste and press hem. Hand sew with catch stitch or herringbone to finish.

Coat hem. Heavy fabric and fur often need two rows of stitching to hold them. If you have to re-stitch part or all of a coat hem, take the opportunity of sewing it more strongly. Baste through hem halfway between bottom and stitching. Fold hem fabric back. Work catch stitch between hem and coat. Replace hem and catch stitch along upper edge.

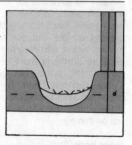

Lining hem. If a lining hem is worn or frayed it is not worth removing the stitches as the lining will suffer even more from the ripping out. Either cut off hem and make a new narrow one or cover original hem with narrow lace oversewn, hemmed or machined along each edge.

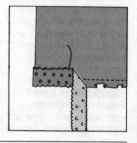

Chiffon hem. A torn or dirty chiffon or silk hem can be trimmed and re-hemmed a little shorter. Roll a narrow hem and hand sew, taking the thread right over the edge. Alternatively, attach narrow hemming foot to the machine which will roll the hem and stitch it.

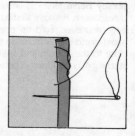

Fluted hem. Soft synthetic jersey sometimes suffers from runs or ladders that begin at the hemline. Remove old stitching and cut off hem, leaving ¼in (6mm) to turn up. Use a small zigzag stitch to machine a new hem. With fabric RS up, fold under ¼in (6mm) and stitch over the fold, pulling fabric quite hard to stretch the jersey. As the hem emerges behind the foot, it will be attractively fluted.

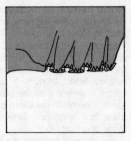

Lingerie hem. If lace edging cannot be repaired, remove it altogether, trim worn edges from the garment and stitch a new hem. Knit fabric can be turned up once and zigzagged or blindstitched to produce a shell effect; or it can be folded over twice and shell stitched by hand. Alternatively, fold up the edge once onto RS and hem narrow lace over it as described for *Lining hem*.

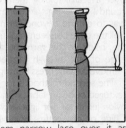

Extension hem. If you need to lengthen the garment, add a band of double fabric. The depth of the finished band depends on the shape of the garment. If it is straight, an extra 2in (5cm) could be added. Select matching or contrasting fabric and cut bias strips twice the finished depth plus ¾in (2cm).

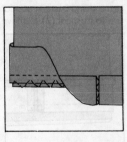

Join pieces if necessary. Fold strip WS together and press. Place on RS of garment with all raw edges even, and baste. Where the ends meet, open out the strip and make the join. This is not easy to reach and it helps to make the join with hand stitching. Press join open, re-fold strip. Stitch around garment ¼in (6mm) from edge, zigzag or oversew to finish. Alternatively, if you can overlock on your machine, use that and work just one row of stitching. Fold band over to extend beyond garment and press lightly.

See also: *Skirt too short*, p. 74; *Sleeves too short*, p. 82.

Faced hem. If so much worn fabric is cut off that none remains to make the hem, additional fabric will have to be used to make a false hem. There are two ways to do this: the first is fairly quick to do and is suitable for trousers, children's clothes and cotton-weight dresses. For both methods, trim garment edges to ½in (13mm) longer than needed. Select fabric such as cotton lawn that is firm but lighter in weight than the garment fabric. Net can be used for lace hems. Wide-width bias binding is available ready-made but is rather coarse and only suitable for clothes made of similar fabric.

Cut strips of fabric on the bias 1½in (4cm) wide and join the ends to make a piece long enough to go around the hem. Fold in one long edge ¼in (6mm) and press. Place bias strip on RS of garment with raw edge of strip ¼in (6mm) inside garment edge. Arrange ends of bias strip to meet over a seam, folding them over and pressing flat. Stitch round hem taking ¼in (6mm) seam on the bias **(1)**. Press bias to extend beyond garment then fold it to the inside. Roll the edge between your fingers until the seam lies just to the inside of the garment, and baste. Baste along upper edge of bias through garment. Slipstitch bias to garment. Remove basting, press hem lightly.

The second method is for coats and clothes made from textured or heavy fabric. Cut and join bias strips of lining or nylon jersey or, for lightweight fabrics, China silk, crepe de Chine or georgette, 1½in (4cm) wide. Fold in both long edges ¼in (6mm) and press. Turn up a narrow hem on garment and herringbone stitch to secure. Press. Arrange bias strip over hem with one edge ¼in (6mm) inside the hemline and baste in position. Slipstitch along both edges of bias to garment **(2)**. Remove basting and press lightly.

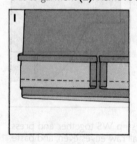 

SEAMS

Seams generally give way because the thread snaps or pulls out due to poor stitching; or because too narrow a seam allowance has frayed; or because the garment is too tight. Before you repair it, try to work out why the seam gave way and if you suspect the third point to be the cause, have a look at the relevant sections in the chapter on *Adjustments for Fit and Comfort*, pp. 89-111.

Most seam repairs can be made quickly and easily, especially if you catch them before they develop into a major sewing job. No matter what was used originally, use only strong thread for re-stitching – core-spun/cotton-wrapped polyester for light and medium fabrics, and linen or button thread for leather, suede, fur and canvas. Always fasten ends of thread securely.

Snapped thread. If one stitch has broken you will probably find that only one thread on one side of the seam has snapped. Leave threads in place and work new stitching to overlap old by at least ¾in (2cm) each end. If sewing by hand, use backstitch to imitate machine stitching. If ends of original stitching can be seen on RS, gently pull them to inside of garment. Press seam.

Split seam. If the seam has split and the thread has broken in several places, it could indicate thread weakness, possibly thread without 'give' used in a stretch or knit fabric. Flatten seam allowances and press. If seam springs up insert a pin at each end. Remove all thread ends on both sides of seam and pull out some

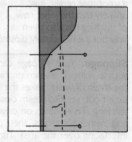

more stitching beyond broken area. If you suspect the break was caused by the original thread it is worth pulling out the entire seam to within 3in (7.5cm) or so of the hem, waistband, cuff or whatever it is that crosses each end. Baste seam and re-stitch, overlapping original stitching at each end by 1½–2¼in (4–6cm). Remove basting. Press seam open.

Inaccessible split seam. If the inside is difficult to reach because of lining or facing, or if you want to keep the article in shape, for instance a chair cover or cushion, the repair must be made by hand from the outside. Try to slide a piece of cardboard under the seam to keep it flat and supported. Using perfectly

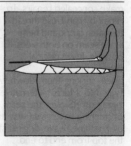

matching thread, start with a knot placed some distance away and bring needle to seam with a series of half backstitches. Work from right to left taking very small stitches alternately in each fabric fold of the seam. Pull thread tight enough to draw edges together and make thread disappear. Overlap original stitching at each end by at least 1in (2.5cm), closing the split. Turn article and repeat stitch, working back the other way, inserting needle between threads already in place. Take needle away from seam to fasten off, and cut off the knot. Press the seam – even if it is a chair cover still on the chair.

Split French seam. The fabric will be lightweight, possibly transparent. Remove any loose ends of thread. Stitch by hand or machine, overlapping original stitching by ¾in (2cm) but starting and finishing at edge of seam for a smoother repair. It is unlikely that the inner row of stitching has also given way but if it has, simply slipstitch by hand.

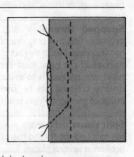

Slippage. Yarn slippage can occur on soft shiny fabrics such as lining. The seam stitching holes become elongated as the strain of wear makes the fabric give way. If garment can be let out, re-stitch seam closer to edge, then undo original stitching. To re-stitch on original seamline, first undo seam and remove threads, then press a strip of soft iron-on interfacing over the area. Turn fabric over and stitch seam following original seamline.

Jeans or welt seam. These seams are usually sewn with multi-thread and multi-needle equipment; fabrics are often thick or tough so it is difficult to make concealed repairs. To repair by hand, use thread to match fabric and hem along seam on both sides. If possible, leave original threads in

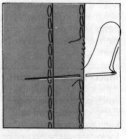

place, sticking them down with spots of fabric adhesive or Fray No More. Alternatively, on a long seam, machine zigzag on RS over the seam, from end to end. If both lines of stitching have given way and you decide to replace them by machine, leave original stitching in place and sew over the top from end to end.

Heavy fabrics. Before re-stitching seams in tough, heavy or closely woven fabrics, provide a reinforced base by pressing a strip of iron-on mending fabric over the area.

Frayed seam. Soft woven fabrics such as wool may fray before thread gives way. Carefully pull all the yarns through to WS, press using a damp cloth, cover area with a strip of soft iron-on interfacing and press again. Turn fabric over and re-stitch seam on top of original stitching. If worn fabric is still visible you might consider applying braid to the outside to cover it.

Points of strain. Seams may begin to come undone at one end, for example at the base of a zipper or other opening, or the top of a pleat. If you can reach inside, place a piece of seam binding or tape where the weakness occurred and re-stitch seam, stopping and fastening off on the tape. Ensure that the same thing

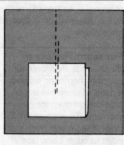

won't happen again by working a hand bar tack with blanketstitch over several threads at end of opening. If inside of garment is too difficult to reach, slipstitch seam from RS and finish with a bar tack.

Faced opening. Sometimes a garment tears from the top of a neckline or sleeve opening where there is no seam. Fold fabric RS together, in line with the opening, and stitch a short dart to take in the worn area. Work a bar tack below end of opening to prevent further wear.

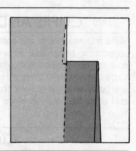

Underarm seam. This is often a weak point due to strain in wear and the effect of perspiration on fabric. In addition, most of the seam is on the bias which allows fabric movement. If stitching has given way, pin sleeve and underarm seam together and re-stitch before shape is lost.

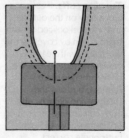

Reinforce area by placing a piece of similar fabric or lining on inside of bodice. Place the straight grain along bodice seam. Pin or baste to garment. Stitch underarm seam again. Trim away surplus fabric and zigzag edge if it frays. This wear may have been caused by the armholes being too tight; you might be well advised to lower the line of stitching at the underarm; see *Armholes too high*, p. 104.

Leather and suede. Repair seams with hand backstitch using a spearpoint needle and waxed button thread. Stitch into holes of original seam if possible. If leather is torn, press a strip of iron-on mending fabric over the area before stitching. If leather seams are soft or weak, place a spot of fabric adhesive or a spot of Fray Check over the thread after stitching.

Fur seam. Remove all thread ends. Reinforce fur edges by hemming around lengths of seam binding or tape placed over the seamline. Re-stitch seam. If original seam was oversewn edge to edge, place tape at edge and re-stitch seam by oversewing edges together, stitching through tape and fabric.

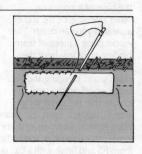

CUFFS AND COLLARS

Slight fraying of cuffs and collars can be controlled with an application of a little Fray Check liquid. Badly worn cuffs can be repaired, but collars are more difficult and have to be turned round or even replaced. If both collar and cuffs are badly worn, it is likely that the garment is nearing the end of its life so think twice before embarking on such a time-consuming repair.

Cuffs

Turning cuffs. If cuffs are worn only on the outside, and you feel obliged to turn them, begin by covering the worn area with seam binding or tape, oversewn or hemmed in place. Remove buttons and stitching and detach cuffs. Turn cuff around and put on opposite sleeve to keep buttonhole correct.

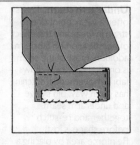

Remove any thread ends and press with both raw edges folded inside cuff. Slip end of sleeve into cuff, match ends and pin. Baste across sleeve. Have cuff with new RS uppermost and stitch ¼in (6mm) inside edge. Turn corners and stitch along cuff ends far enough to overlap ends of original stitching. If the buttonhole looks rough, place a small piece of iron-on interfacing underneath and re-stitch over old buttonhole. Replace buttons.

Soft cuffs. Sometimes a too soft interfacing will cause early wear on blouse and dress cuffs. First the cuff appears wrinkled, and then the fabric will wear out along the wrinkles. Catch it before it wears through. Remove buttons and stitching around outer edge of cuff; press edges flat. Cut a piece of soft iron-on interfacing slightly smaller than the cuff and insert it with adhesive against outer layer of cuff. If the original interfacing has come adrift, either smooth it back into position or remove it altogether and use

medium-weight interfacing instead. Cut a slit in the interfacing so that it fits around the buttonhole. Baste layers of cuff together, turn in outer edges, baste and press, then baste pressed edges together. Slipstitch together, replace any original edge stitching and sew on button.

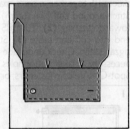

Worn edges. A watch or bracelet may cause a cuff to wear along the edge. Remove stitching along lower edge and press cuff flat. Cut a strip of soft iron-on interfacing and press against outer edge of cuff. Cut off edge to remove worn part. Fold in ¼in (6mm) on outer cuff and press. Fold inner cuff edge to meet it. Baste together. Machine stitch to match original edge stitching, overlapping it by at least ⅜in (1cm). You need not necessarily shorten other cuff to match; it depends whether repair is obvious or not.

Worn edges – narrow cuff. If cuff design is unsuitable for shortening, cover worn edge by applying bias binding. This is available ready-folded in a wide variety of colours. Check the width when folded over the edge of the cuff. If it does not cover the worn part, trim a little off the cuff. Remove buttons.

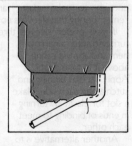

Fold in end of binding, wrap around cuff edge evenly and baste. On reaching the far end, trim binding and fold under. Stitch along edge of binding with cuff RS up, using straight, zigzag or decorative stitch. Fasten ends neatly. Check underside of cuff. If any part of edge has not been stitched, fill in with hand stitching. Alternatively, stitch binding with small neat hemming or oversewing stitches on both sides of the cuff. Replace buttons.

If you use a contrast colour binding, see whether you can also feature it somewhere else on the garment to make the repair less obvious.

Badly worn cuffs. Provided the rest of the garment is good, remove the cuffs altogether and make new ones. Use an old cuff as a pattern and cut out two pieces of iron-on interfacing, adding ¼in (6mm) all round. Place on WS of new fabric and press. Cut around edge. Cut two more fabric pieces. Fold in ¼in (6mm) along upper edges. Pin pieces RS together in pairs, matching folded edges carefully. Stitch around cuff ¼in (6mm) from edge **(1)**. Snip corners toward stitching **(2)**. Turn RS out and press. Insert sleeve end into cuff and baste **(3)**. Stitch in place using straight or zigzag stitch. Check underside and fill in with hand sewing if necessary. Make buttonholes and attach buttons, Velcro Spot-Ons/Velcoin fasteners, or decorative snap fasteners.

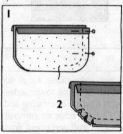

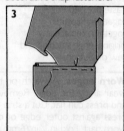

Full sleeves. If sleeves are soft and gathered you may prefer to dispense with cuffs in favour of narrow elastic. Cut off worn cuffs. Make a dart into the wrist where the opening is, cut off bulky facings etc., and make a casing wide enough to take elastic and stitch. Measure elastic, remembering that sleeve is now shorter, and insert.

If you prefer sleeves three-quarter or elbow length, turn and stitch a narrow hem and apply a casing above it to take elastic. Apply flat bias binding and stitch along each side. Make a slot for elastic by turning in ends of binding to meet each other.

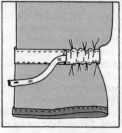

Another alternative is to apply several rows of shirring elastic above the hem; see *Shirring elastic*, p. 42.

Sports sleeve. A shirt sleeve can easily be converted to a rolled up sleeve. Cut off worn cuffs. Fold a narrow hem and stitch. Stitch up opening by overlapping it and topstitching. Fold up sleeve several times onto the outside and press. If you can, shorten the sleeve by cutting off 3¼in (8cm)

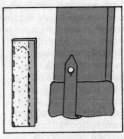

before making the hem. This provides fabric to make straps as follows: cut two pieces of soft Fold-a-Band, 5½in (14cm) long and press to WS of surplus fabric. Cut out, adding ⅜in (1cm) seam all round. Fold strap RS inside along perforations. Stitch beside edge of Fold-a-Band, stitching a point at one end. Trim points. Turn straps RS out and press. Make a buttonhole at the point or attach a decorative snap fastener or Spot-On/Velcoin fastener. Place strap on inside of sleeve, level with elbow and in line with position of original opening. Stitch a rectangle to secure. Roll up sleeve onto RS, bring strap over and fasten to sleeve with button or other half of snap fastener or Spot-On/Velcoin fastener.

Collars

On shirts with stiff collars, it is the fold at the back of the neck that most often wears out.

Collar band. If the shirt has a band and a separate pointed section and provided the band is not worn, remove the stitching holding the pointed section in place and withdraw the collar. Press the band, remove ends of thread and re-stitch, matching up original stitching at ends. Neatly finish off the ends.

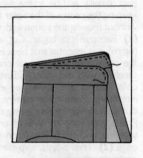

Turning. Look underneath the collar before ripping it off; it cannot be turned if there are pockets for stiffeners or any random reinforcing stitching. Remove button. Using a fabric marking pen, make at least four strokes from collar onto shirt. Remove stitching along base of neckband. Do not press or over-handle the shirt neck edge or it will stretch beyond belief. Remove thread ends from collar and fold in half to press the halfway point on the neck edge.

With folded edges even, extend pen marks over onto the other edge. Insert shirt neck edge between collar edges.

Match ends and pen marks, and pin. Try to place collar edges on top of old stitching marks. Baste close to edge through all layers. Remove pins. On inside of neck, slipstitch or hem along edge of collar.

With collar underside up, machine stitch close to basted edge. Fasten off neatly at each end. Remove basting. Press. Make a new buttonhole on side of band where button had been. Oversew edges of old buttonhole in other end of band. Sew button in place on top of old buttonhole.

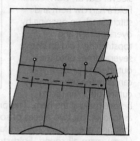

New collar. If you are an experienced sewer, you can replace a collar as well as cuffs, in colours and fabrics that contrast with the old ones. Make at least four marks between collar and shirt using fabric marking pen. Undo collar stitching, removing collar and band as one. Do not press or handle neck edge of shirt or it will stretch. Press old collar flat and cut in half. Place one half on paper folded double. The next move is tricky because the old collar was heat-set into its shape during manufacture, but you now need it to be flat in order to draw round it and you are also going to dispense with the separate band. Begin by flattening neck edge of band, pin to the paper or secure with tape. Outline lower edge at ends. Next, flatten upper part of collar and pin to the paper, releasing lower part but keeping the centre of the collar on the fold of the paper and without moving the round end. Outline upper part of collar **(1)**. Remove old collar. Cut around outline adding ¼in (6mm). It is essential that neck edge of new collar is exactly the same length as original one, so check paper pattern carefully with old collar, adjusting it if necessary. Outline collar points and outer edge and cut out in iron-on interfacing. Place collar pattern on doubled fabric and cut out with straight grain running down centre back of collar. Press interfacing to WS of one piece. Place collars RS together and stitch ¼in (6mm) from edge, omitting neck edge **(2)**. Trim points, snip curves, turn collar RS out and

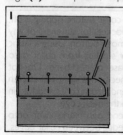

ease out points using a bodkin. Press. Turn in ¼in (6mm) along neck edges and press again. Fold collar to neck. Shape and Press once again. Note that interfaced side is the under collar in folded position. Transfer pen marks accurately from old collar pieces to new collar.

Matching the marks, insert shirt neck between collar edges. Baste from end to end. Slipstitch or hem along edge on RS of shirt. With inside of collar uppermost, machine stitch close to fold and all round edge of collar and band **(3)**. Fasten off neatly. Press. Make a buttonhole in one end of band and sew a button in place on other end.

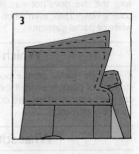

PATCHING

An additional piece of material is used to conceal a hole, rip or thin place where the less conspicuous darn would be inadequate. The purpose of the patch is to renovate the garment and prolong its life. If the garment is torn, cut or ripped, draw the edges together before patching, using fishbone stitch or iron-on interfacing. If the garment has worn thin, the area should first be darned. Patches must be bigger than the worn or weakened area or the edges will provide an immediate point of weakness for further wear. Trace the area and make a paper pattern. Small holes and tears can often be patched inconspicuously; large areas carrying a patch are almost bound to be visible. This point might influence the type of patch you choose.

What fabric?

The material available will influence the method you choose. If you made the garment originally there is a chance that you can patch inconspicuously using some of the leftover fabric. Or even if the garment was bought, see if there is a piece of fabric that could be used as a patch, for example a pocket bag could be cut off and replaced with plain fabric; the back of a pleat near the waist could be cut; small pieces could be cut from facings. On the outside there may be a patch pocket that could be taken off or, more drastically, perhaps sleeves could be shortened to provide patching fabric. Ready-made patches and pieces of patching fabric are available in a range of fabrics including suede, leather, cotton, denim and corduroy, and in a variety of shades. Some are sew-on, others iron-on. The alternative is to use contrasting fabric. It should be the same weight or heavier than the garment, fairly non-fray, and in keeping with the rest of the garment. Try to plan other features in the contrasting fabric to create a design rather than an obvious patch.

With the exception of ready-made patches, always wash the fabric or soak it for a while and iron before use. Make sure the dye does not run. In fact, it is not wise to risk putting heavy reds, even when they are bought patches, on white or pastel garments.

Which side?

It depends mainly on the position of the hole and the strength of patch needed. If there is a design to match, you can see better what you are doing if the patch is applied to RS of the garment.

What stitching?

Machine stitching is stronger, provided ends are fastened off properly, but it will show. Hand sewing is less visible and you can see what you are doing more clearly, especially if the patch is small. However, the deciding factor may well be whether or not the area is accessible by machine. Use straight or small zigzag machine stitches, hand oversewing or hemming, or herringbone stitch for a flatter but less strong finish.

Which patch?

The type of patch is usually determined by the position of the hole, or maybe by the type of fabric. Select the method that suits both.

Emergency patch.
Although supposed to be a temporary remedy it may well outlast the garment. If it starts to become detached see whether you could simply add stitching rather than replacing it altogether. For a thin place, rip or tear, apply the patch to WS of garment. If you need to cover a hole apply

the patch to RS and replace it as soon as possible.

Cut a piece of fabric at least ¾in (2cm) bigger than the extent of the rip. Round off corners. Press Bondaweb/ Wonder-Under to WS. Peel off paper and place on pressing surface, adhesive uppermost. Place garment WS down onto patch. Smooth down loose yarns, draw together edges of rip with fishbone stitch. Press gently. Cover with damp cloth and press thoroughly. Leave to cool before wearing.

The above method is a good way of repairing chair covers and upholstery. Do not remove the cover; carefully insert a patch, adhesive side up, through the tear. Stitch edges together if necessary. Press as described.

Bobble patch. A small darn or patch can be concealed by attaching a bunch of two or three pompoms or tassels made from knitting yarn.

Embroidery patch. Before cutting a patch to size, decorate it with an embroidered motif. You may need to make more than one motif to produce a balanced design. Alternatively, small darns or stains can be covered with embroidery. Plan a design and embroider in stitching or narrow ribbon.

Darned patch. For soft fabrics with texturing on RS, cover hole with a piece of fabric and anchor with basting tape. Using yarns from the fabric and feeling the edge beneath, darn back and forth over edge of hole extending for ¼in (6mm) each side. Trim away excess patch.

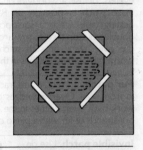

Drop-in patch. This is for bulky fabrics that do not fray. Trim hole to a regular shape. Make a tracing of hole and cut out patch. Drop patch into hole and machine stitch with a wide running zigzag to straddle the join.

Crotch patch. Tight jeans often wear between the legs. Undo the crotch seam from leg seams to base of pocket. Pin pieces of denim WS down over worn area. Fold under all edges except crotch, and baste. Machine edges twice in thread to match other stitching. Pin crotch seam together and re-stitch, trimming off

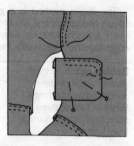

surplus patching fabric. Darn worn area from the inside, occasionally catching the new fabric in the stitching. If there is a hole, trim it, turn under the edge and hem to new fabric.

Elbow patch. Darn the hole or thin place. Use oval shapes of suede, leather or corduroy, or buy them ready-made; some of these have punched stitching holes, some are padded. Iron-on patches should be sewn as well to take the strain of the elbow. If you make your own leather patches, punch holes

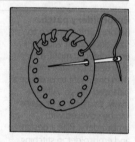

around the edge with the tool that comes with a pack of eyelets, or use a woodworking bradawl or a large needle. Place patch in position on RS of garment, secure with basting tape. Using a spearpoint needle and waxed and doubled button thread, sew around the edge through holes; use oversewing or stab stitch. Make it more secure by working back over stitches in the opposite direction.

Fur patch. Trim hole and trace it. Cut a patch and drop it in from WS. Oversew edges of the skin or backing, then work back over stitches in the other direction. On RS ease out strands of fur with a pin to conceal join.

Invisible patch. Use on good clothes where patch would show, and on lingerie. Identical fabric must be used. Place fabric RS up on RS of garment, and pin. Turn under all edges and baste. Slipstitch all round. On WS trim hole to ¼in (6mm) from stitching, oversew or blanketstitch raw edge.

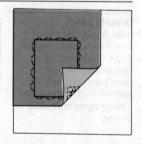

Jeans pocket patch. One corner often wears out and is simpler to patch before it becomes a hole. Undo stitching around worn corner and lift it free. Cut a square patch large enough to cover worn area. If fabric has only worn thin, place patch underneath and attach as described under *Emergency patch*, p.58. To cover a hole, place patch RS up on top of pocket, and pin. Fold under raw edges. Press. Stitch close to edge by machine or, if the area is difficult to reach, slipstitch or hem along edges by hand **(1)**. On the underside, trim away worn area ¾in (2cm) from stitching. Fold under, press and stitch again or, if fabric is heavy, oversew raw edge and backstitch ⅜in (1cm) from first row of stitching. Finish by trimming outer edge of patch evenly with pocket, fold under, baste to trousers and re-stitch **(2)**. Either stitch by machine or hem along the fold and add some hand backstitches to imitate original stitching.

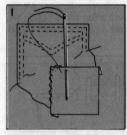

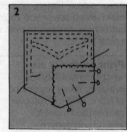

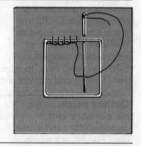

Knitted patch. For holes and thin places. Using small needles and contrasting yarn, knit plain patches in garter stitch or striped ones in stocking/stockinet stitch. Trim hole, place patch underneath, RS up, and blanketstitch around edge of hole to join to knitting.

Linen patch. For household goods and work clothes. Cut a square of fabric, fold in all edges onto RS and press. Place over hole on WS, pin or baste in position. Stitch all round close to edge. On RS cut almost to stitching at corners, trim worn fabric to within ⅜in (1cm) of stitching. Fold under raw edges, press. stitch close to fold.

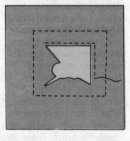

Pocket patch. In various places such as thighs and around the knee area, any iron-on or conventional patch can be covered with a useful pocket. Mend a thin place with a darn; and a hole by applying a patch on WS following instructions given on previous page for *Linen patch*. Make a paper pattern for a large patch

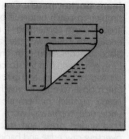

pocket allowing for seams all round and 1¼in (3cm) for top hem. Press Fold-a-Band to upper edge on WS. Turn in all other edges and press. Fold down top edge and press. Pin in position over patch on RS of garment. Stitch around three sides. Fasten corners securely. If you are an experienced sewer you could add a flap and a button and buttonhole, or you can even make a poacher's pocket with a pleat in it.

Print patch. For use where identical fabric is available. Take a large piece of fabric, hold it RS up over garment and move it around until pattern matches, then pin it in place. From WS mark extent of hole using pins. On RS trim patch, turn under edges and hold with basting tape to keep pattern matched.

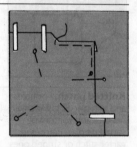

Stitch all round, close to edge. On WS trim hole to within ⅜in (1cm) of stitching, fold under and stitch.

Quilted patch. Back a piece of fabric with wadding/batting and muslin/lawn. Hand quilt a simple design such as diamonds or initials, using running stitch. Trim patch to a neat shape and remove padding from the edge. Fold in edge of fabric and backing and baste. Place patch over hole, baste. Slipstitch

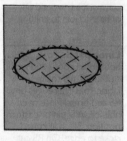

around edge to secure. On WS trim hole level with raw edge of patch and oversew together. On outer garments it is well worth adding other quilted patches to form a complete design. These patches can be made larger and will provide warmth as well as decoration.

Stocking patch. For large holes in knitting; trim edge, make a tracing of the hole and cut out a piece of knitting slightly bigger – use a good area of another old garment. Drop patch into hole. On WS join edges of knitting with blanketstitch.

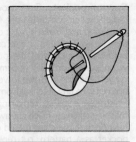

Topstitch patch. If mend cannot be hidden, make a feature of it by using contrasting fabric, and cutting decorative shapes such as diamonds and hexagons. Avoid triangles as the corners are too acute. Press soft iron-on interfacing to WS. To form a design, cut out several shapes, one of which must be big enough to cover the hole. Turn in and press all edges. Place patches in position and pin or secure with basting tape. Stitch around edge of each with two rows of contrasting stitching. On WS trim away hole to within ¼in (6mm) of stitching and oversew raw edge.

Trouser pocket patch. Coins often wear a hole in the lower part of the pocket. Patch using calico, strong cotton or tailor's pocketing. Cut a piece 1¼in (3cm) wider than the pocket and more than twice the depth needed to cover the hole. For extra strength cut fabric double this size and fold the fabric in half.

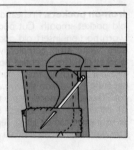

Trim edges of hole, fold ⅛in (3mm) onto outside and press. Pin patch in place, wrapping it round bottom of pocket. Fold under raw edges, pin or baste. Stitch along each fold to attach patch to one layer of pocket, hemming by hand. Trim sides of patch parallel with, but clear of, the pocket and stitch together, curving bottom corners. Oversew or hem around hole to new fabric.

Alternatively buy sew-on or iron-on replacement pockets, which are available in a choice of fabrics. Select the one that most closely resembles the worn pocket.

Sew-on pockets. Open trousers and turn inside out. Iron old pocket smooth. Measure 4in (10cm) down from base of waistband and make a mark on pocket with fabric marking pen. Draw a curved line to connect this mark with a point below the bottom of the pocket opening, taking off the worn part. Add ⅝in (1.5cm) seam allowance, cut along curved line and remove lower portion of pocket **(1)**. (Do not remove any stitching from the remaining pocket piece.) Finish raw edge on remaining pocket piece by pinking or machine stitching. Place cut-away section of old pocket over new pocket, matching folded edges and bottoms. Using old pocket as a pattern, cut replacement pocket 1¼in (3cm) larger. Finish raw edges of new pocket by pinking or machine stitching. Slip new pocket inside the old and baste in place. Before stitching, make sure pocket is smooth. Stitch a ⅝in (1.5cm) seam starting just below the pocket opening **(2)**. Finally, backstitch at the beginning and the end to secure the stitching.

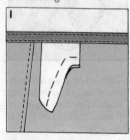
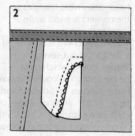

Iron-on pockets. Preheat dry iron at 'Cotton' setting. Iron old pocket smooth. Cut pocket off straight across, above worn portion. Insert old pocket into replacement, making sure white strip completely overlaps cut edges of old pocket **(1)**. Cover entire pocket with a pressing cloth to prevent scorching. Press iron firmly on white strip for 10 seconds. Move iron slowly with pressure over entire strip for 30 seconds more. Allow to cool. Turn over and repeat on other side. Test security by trying to lift edge of white strip. If edge can be lifted, repeat pressing. Stitch from join to lower edge in line with old pocket **(2)**. Trim off surplus.

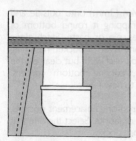
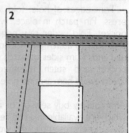

Tweed patch. For thick, soft fabrics that give. Baste fabric over hole or thin place on RS of garment. Work herringbone stitch all round over edge. For a thin place, catch new fabric from time to time on WS. For a hole, trim away to within ¾in (2cm) of stitching and herringbone over edge.

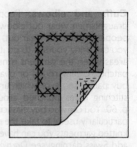

Velvet patch. Also for velour and other soft fabrics with pile. Trim hole to a rectangle, snip into corners, turn under edges and baste. Trace hole and cut a patch, adding ⅜in (1cm) all round. From WS place patch in hole, fold back edges and baste to fit hole. Join patch to garment with hand slipstitch, taking very small stitches from each fold in turn.

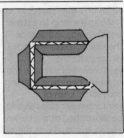

Zigzag patch. A strong repair for use on bulky fabrics. Baste patch in position on RS. Work a line of long zigzag just inside edge to secure. Starting in middle of patch, work rows of zigzag back and forth covering patch and overlapping raw edges. The worn fabric will be firmly stitched on WS.

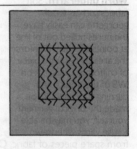

REINFORCEMENTS

As a result of work or a particular activity some parts of garments may be subject to abnormal wear. It is worth reinforcing these parts when the garment is new or at least when wear begins to show. See also *Patching.* p. 57.

Pockets. One or more pockets in dungarees and overalls may be subject to hard wear. If the top corners usually tear, either make strong bar tacks with waxed button thread at each corner or hem a strip of seam binding, tape or mending fabric across the corner. If the stitching across the bottom breaks, stitch round the entire pocket again. On a new garment add this second row before it is worn.

Cuffs and elbows. People such as architects and draughtsmen wear out elbows, and perhaps there are still people whose cuffs wear out, like those of Dickens' clerks. If you can bring yourself to do it, it is easier to reinforce these areas when the garment is new. You can make your own patches, cutting round or oval shapes to avoid corners, or buy packs, some of which are iron-on, while others have stitching holes punched around the edge. See *Patching*, p. 60. You can also buy elasticized stretch patches which are particularly useful to take the movement of the elbows. For knitted garments you can have patches applied or you could add Swiss darning; see *Darning*, P. 19. Sleeves should have strips of leather, suede or corduroy hemmed to the cuffs.

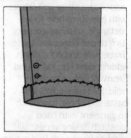

Wrap the strip to extend equally inside and outside the sleeve. It is difficult to pin or baste the reinforcement so make use of fusible hemming web and then stitch. Ends of reinforcement strips should be slipstitched or oversewn end to end level with the cuff opening.

Worn underarm. Soft fabrics such as wool georgette can easily have the fibres pulled out of line at points of strain. Reinforce the area by basting a piece of chiffon or China silk on WS of the bodice and darning it by hand. If you made the original garment yourself, you may be able to use yarns withdrawn

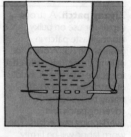

from spare pieces of fabric. Otherwise darn with soft matt thread or a strand of embroidery silk/floss. Trim off surplus inside garment.

Underarm and crotch seams. Place a piece of bias binding, pressed flat, over the seam stitching around the curve of the garment. Stitch in place using a stretch stitch or slight zigzag following the original stitching. If the thread in a crotch seam habitually breaks, replace with a stitch that stretches.

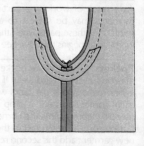

Pleats that tear. If stitching gives way replace it but place a folded piece of tape or seam binding under the end of the stitching. You might also consider making the stitching shorter to avoid the strain being in the same place. Any other pleats on the garment will also have to be altered correspondingly.

If the fabric is torn, repair it by darning, then cover with a thread arrowhead worked with buttonhole twist or embroidery thread. Mark out a triangle in fabric marking pen. Starting with a knot on WS, bring needle through to RS at bottom left of triangle. Insert needle a fraction to the right of top of triangle, using a stabbing movement **(1)**. Take needle through to WS and bring out slightly to left. Insert needle at bottom right of triangle **(2)**; bring it up at bottom left, a fraction inside the first stitch. Insert at top right, bring out at top left. Continue in this way, following the marked outline, until the triangle has been filled as shown **(3)**. An easier alternative is to cut triangular patches from suede or corduroy and machine stitch or oversew in position **(4)**. All pleats must be treated in the same way.

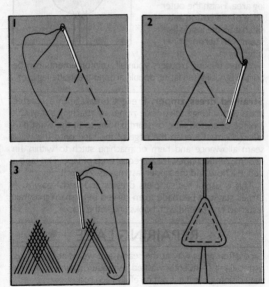

Skirts that 'seat'. Not all fabrics return to shape, and straight, knitted, or unlined skirts will nearly always 'seat'. Insert a piece of lining in the back extending from the base of the zipper to well below thigh level. Conventional lining material is not really strong enough, so use firm nylon jersey if possible.

With skirt WS out, lift the seam allowances and baste the additional material with rows of stitching, smoothing the material tightly over the skirt. Cut away surplus fabric and trim the edges with pinking shears to avoid a ridge. Attach lining material to skirt seam allowances using backstitch or machine stitching.

Trouser thighs. Abrasion of the fabric on the inner thigh area cannot be prevented, but it helps to attach a piece of cotton fabric to the crotch seam, extending it down the inside leg area. Finish the outer edge of the cotton and catch it to the inside leg seam with herringbone stitch.

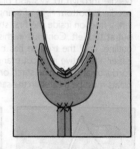

When making trousers yourself, reinforcements can be built in by using the fabric double around the inside leg area.

Strained dress zipper. Prevent breakage in a waisted dress with a long back or side zipper by attaching a stay. Cut a piece of cotton tape or seam binding to fit the waist plus 20in (50cm). Overlap the edge of the tape onto the waist seam allowance and hem or machine stitch to within 1in (2.5cm) of the zipper, leaving equal ends of tape. The tape is tied in a bow and the zipper fastens easily over it.

This is useful for strapless dresses and bridal gowns. A firmer stay can be made from curved petersham/grosgrain fastened end to end with hooks under the zipper.

REPAIRING LACE

Lace often gives way at the seams and wears at the edges, especially if frequently washed. Antique or handmade lace may disintegrate if it is not carefully repaired.

Holes. Small holes can be repaired by placing net beneath the hole and oversewing around the edge. Larger holes are best mended with another piece of lace; the design may not be the same as the original but use lace of the same type and weight and the repair will not show too much. A third alternative, if several parts are worn, is to press Bondaweb/Wonder-Under to WS of a piece of lace, cut out motifs, remove the paper backing and press them in position.

Seams. Hairline or narrow seams can be mended by placing soft net under the lace and re-stitching with oversewing or machine zigzag. A plain open seam should have a strip of net placed on each side before re-stitching.

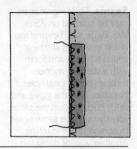

Edges. Place a piece of soft net under the worn area. Mend lace by oversewing remaining original strands to the net. Use sewing thread for fine lace, embroidery thread for heavy types. The stitching may be done by machine using a small zigzag, although in time this may cause further tearing if the lace is fine or old. On WS,

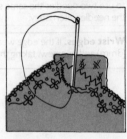

trim away surplus net. If lace edging is worn in several places, remove it and replace by slipstitching new lace in position. If a lace garment is badly worn, bind the entire edge with satin after backing the area with net.

Lace skirt. If a skirt hem is worn and torn all round, undo any remaining hem and press. Fold up ⅛in (3mm) more than original hem, baste and press. Baste skirt lining to skirt and hem in place to reinforce and help prevent further wear. If the lining is not long enough or not the right size, remove it and replace it with a new one.

MENDING LEATHER GLOVES

Use a small size spearpoint needle and core-spun/cotton-wrapped polyester thread, or button or linen thread for heavy leather. Wax the thread but use it singly.

Holes. Patch with a piece of similar leather. Trim the hole evenly and blanketstitch around the edge. Cut a patch that will fit into the hole and blanketstitch around it. Place in position and attach by oversewing, picking up the blanketstitch from both edges.

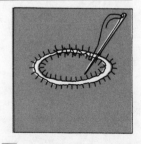

Seams. The original seam may be stitched on RS or WS. Begin well beyond the break in the old stitching and stitch back and forth with a stabbing motion, through the original holes if possible. Turn the glove and stitch back again in the same way through the same holes to complete the stitching. Another way of doing this is

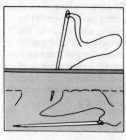

to use two needles the same size and stitch once only, using the needles alternately.

Wrist edges. If the edge wears out, trim neatly, fold in 1/8in (3mm) and oversew, taking the thread over the edge.

RENOVATIONS AND IMPROVEMENTS

Something quite simple will often update or alter a garment sufficiently to bring it back into service. Many people are hesitant about tampering with ready-made clothes but none of the suggestions outlined are extensive; some are quite minor but will correct an irritating feature. In addition to the basic changes described you can add individuality by using braids, edgings and contrasting fabrics where appropriate.

General hints

Also read the section on *Adjustments for Fit and Comfort*, pp. 89–111, in case the problem is one of fit rather than style.

1. Do not undo old stitching until you have marked or even stitched the new seamline.

2. *Never* cut the garment until you have double checked that you are not cutting off too much – remember, seam and hem allowances must be added to your new line.

3. If you are uncertain about the size of the alteration, go to a garment that you are happy wearing and measure it up. This is particularly good advice when deciding on skirt and trouser lengths, but remember that width around the hemline is also important.

4. Mark new seamlines on WS using tailor's chalk or fabric marking pen and always use a ruler for straight seams. Curves are more difficult to draw; try making a dotted line instead of a continuous line.

5. When unstitching the garment, if the fabric frays badly or seems to be very limp without its rows of industrial stitching, make use of fusible products such as soft iron-on Vilene, Wundaweb, Bondaweb/Pellon, Stitch Witchery, Wonder-Under.

6. Always check the lengths of corresponding seams such as shoulders, side and sleeve seams, and skirt and trouser seams.

7. The old stitching marks can be a useful guide so press only lightly when sewing but press well on completion.

TROUSERS

Legs too flared. Undo hems and press. If hems were held with Wundaweb/Stitch Witchery pull the fabric gently. A little methylated spirits/denatured alcohol applied with a piece of soft cotton will dissolve any web left on fabric. Decide on amount to be taken off each leg. Make tailor's chalk or fabric pen marks at hemline to take one third at inside leg seam and two thirds at outside leg. This will ensure that the legs hang together in wear. Draw a straight line from hem points to join original stitching no higher than thigh level and below any seam pockets. Undo existing seam stitching for about 3in (8cm) above and below the point at which new and old seamlines meet. Press unstitched areas. Stitch new seams

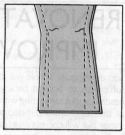

smoothly from hem to thigh, running gently into old stitching line and overlapping by ¾in (2cm). Trim away surplus fabric beside new stitching, leaving same width seam allowance as originally. Press new seams. Open seams should be zigzagged or oversewn if fabric frays. Finish welt or double-stitched seams by copying method used on original as far as possible. Turn up hem along original fold, baste, press and re-stitch.

Legs too long. Undo hems and press out crease marks. Measure new length and mark on inside and outside leg seams on RS. Turn surplus up inside trousers and hold in place with pins inserted vertically. Try on the trousers wearing shoes and look in a mirror, adjusting pins if necessary. An ideal trouser hem slopes down so that leg is ⅜in (1cm) longer at back. Baste along fold, remove pins and press. Trim off surplus fabric. Hem may be between ⅝in (1.5cm) and 2in (5cm). Finish raw edge if fabric frays, baste flat and sew with herringbone stitch or catch stitch or use Wundaweb/Stitch Witchery and press well. Press hems and replace leg creases.

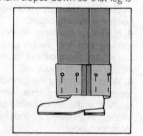

SKIRTS

Flare too full. Undo hem for 6in (15cm) on each side of all seams. With skirt WS out, pin out the necessary reduction at hem, taking an equal amount from each seam. Draw lines from hem to thigh level, finishing below zipper. Baste seams on new lines and try on if possible. Adjust if

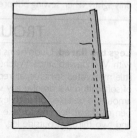

necessary. Stitch seams from hem to thigh, overlapping original stitching and following it accurately for ¾in (2cm). Undo old stitching. Trim seam allowances, press seams open and zigzag edges. Turn up hem on original hemline, baste, press and stitch. Press.

Lining too full. If a lined skirt is narrowed as described above, reduce width of lining. Take new stitching a little higher on each seam to keep a close fit. Sew seams with a zigzag or overlock stitch only and press to one side. If lining has seams to correspond with those in skirt, reduce them equally. If skirt has four seams but lining only two, you will probably find it is already narrower than the skirt and needs reducing at sides only.

Lining too long. Lining hem may be uneven so this is a chance to straighten it. Hang up skirt from waist inside out. Insert pins in lining evenly ¾in (2cm) above bottom edge of skirt. Cut off surplus lining close to pins, removing pins. If any old hem stitching remains remove it. Press lining. Turn up and stitch new lining hem, turning a narrow fold twice, basting, finishing either with hand hemming or with machine stitching.

Uneven hem. Measure skirt at a point where length is correct and make a note. Undo skirt hem, remove all thread and press to remove marks. Measure length required and put a pin or chalk mark on RS. Mark a line all round at this level. Use a long ruler or hem marker and measure evenly from the ground. If this is not possible, lay skirt on a table, folded carefully along centre front and centre back, and measure evenly from waist. Turn up skirt on marked line, baste and press. Trim surplus to an even width, zigzag edge and finish with hand catch stitch or machining. Press.

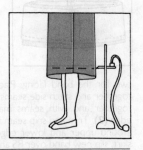

Hemline shows. To remove marks, try pressing lightly on RS over a damp cloth with skirt on a folded towel. On WS slide the iron, still using the cloth, under edge of hem to try to steam out marks. If this is not successful remove stitching and press skirt on both sides with hem held free, brushing fabric while warm. If marks have not disappeared after fabric has been left to cool, baste hem back into position and finish with several rows of machine stitching to cover them. If you successfully remove old marks, re-stitch hem by hand. Keep thread loose and press fold if necessary but do not rest iron on hem edge.

Skirt too long. Follow method described on previous page for *Uneven hem* but when cutting off surplus, leave enough to make a hem 2–2½in (5–6cm) deep on a straight or A-line skirt, ⅜–¾in (1–2cm) if flared.

Skirt too short. Using fabric of a similar weight, lengthen skirt with a shaped band. Plan another feature such as patch pockets, belt, cuffs or bow to complete the design. Fold skirt RS out along centre front and centre back and place on folded paper. Place centre front against fold of paper, smooth out skirt and outline it around hem as far as side seam. Remove skirt and complete shape of band below the line, making it the desired finished depth and adding ⅝in (1.5cm) seam allowance above, below and at side seam **(1)**. Repeat for back of skirt. Fold fabric and cut each pattern twice against the fold, making four pieces in all, two for the band and

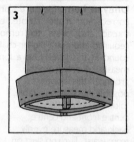

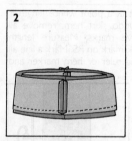

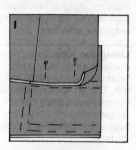

two for the band facing. Place front and back bands RS together and stitch side seams. Press open. With bands RS together and with seams matching, stitch around lower edge **(2)**. Trim and snip seam allowance, turn RS out, baste around upper and lower edges and press. Undo hem of skirt, slip new band over RS and baste with seamline on old hem fold **(3)**. Press edges then stitch around skirt. Trim and zigzag edges if fabric frays. Press so band extends below skirt. A line of topstitching above seam and above hem edge will make it appear a more permanent feature.

A second method involves cutting skirt and inserting a single fabric shaped band above hem. Use skirt to make a pattern as described above but marking a line higher up and making pattern below it. Cut out on single fabric and make up band. Cut skirt ⅝in (1.5cm) below marked insert line.

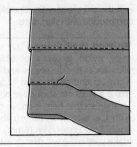

Fold up the seam allowance and press. Slip band under edge, match seams, baste and topstitch. Fold up seam allowance on lower edge of band. Press. Replace lower part of skirt by slipping upper edge under finished edge of band, basting and topstitching. Press.

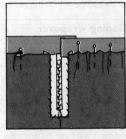

Adding a lining. If an unlined skirt needs a lining the easiest way to do it is to remove the elastic from a half slip, dye the slip to match and drop it into the skirt.

Pin slip around skirt waist on WS, turn under raw edge and slipstitch or hem to bottom of waistband. Cut into slip along zipper, zigzag raw edges and hem to zipper tapes. This may well be less expensive than buying lining fabric and it is less work.

However, if you prefer a conventional lining it is not difficult to make one. There is no need to make a paper pattern, simply mark shape for back and front directly onto folded lining material as follows. With RS out fold skirt along centre front and centre back. Place front against fold in lining fabric, smooth out skirt and outline with tailor's chalk around hem and along side seam to hip level. Mark waist position at base of band. Remove skirt. Extend side seam in a straight line, draw waist as a slight curve. Cut ⅝in (1.5cm) beyond outline. Repeat for the back, placing centre back to selvages of lining and leaving a ⅝in (1.5cm) seam allowance. Mark length of zipper plus 1¼in (3cm) at appropriate seam. With lining RS together, stitch and press seams, leaving opening for zipper. Turn up a hem ¾in (2cm) deep and stitch. Fold in zipper edges ¾in (2cm) and press, snipping even with top of seam stitching so that it lies flat. Slip lining inside skirt, WS together, matching seams and pin. Gather surplus at waist or fold into small tucks over skirt darts. Baste in place. Fold under raw edge and hem lining to base of waistband; hem lining to zipper tapes.

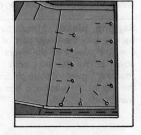

If the skirt is very fitted, make darts instead of gathers to correspond with skirt darts.

Knitted skirt lining. Place skirt on double layer of lining using nylon jersey if possible. Add ⅝in (1.5cm) seam allowance at side seams and cut out. Stitch lining seams. Turn up and stitch a 1in (2.5cm) hem or trim edge and make a machine shell edge hem. Slip lining inside skirt and arrange so that hem is above skirt hem; baste around waist with top edge ¼in (6mm) above base of elastic or waist finish. Fold under ¼in (6mm), ease onto knitting and hem. Make sure lining will stretch with skirt by leaving a small loop of thread between stitches every ¾in (2cm).

Gaping wrapover. This is a common fault in skirts and dresses, and is caused by sitting a great deal or by the back skirt being too short or too narrow. A simple solution is to fasten and baste the wrap, starting at hem with edges even. Topstitch from hem to hip level, leaving sufficient opening above. If wrapover panel was originally unfastened, sew buttons right to hem, spacing them to match those above so that it gives the impression of always having been a button-through style. If in addition you can let out the side seams it will help improve the hang.

Pleats that open. If pleats do not hang together it could be that they were not constructed correctly, that the skirt is tight or that the distance between waist and top of pleat is wrong for the figure. The solution is to lengthen or shorten the pleat stitching.

Put on skirt in order to decide which would be best; check with other pleated skirts you have. Mark a new pleat point with a pin above or below original. If you propose to shorten stitching, look inside skirt to make sure backing piece extends far enough. With skirt WS out, fold each pleat to reveal stitching, press flat. Pin and baste for longer seams, or make chalk marks for shorter seams. If pleats were stitched from outside, mark or baste on RS. If pleats were topstitched and also sewn inside, remove topstitching before you begin. Start well above marked point, sew to the point, turn and stitch back again to overlap old stitching by 1½in (4cm). Remove any unwanted stitching. Press pleats. See also *Pleats that tear*, p. 67.

Sagging pleats. Manufacturers often economize by backing only the lower part of an inverted pleat so that in time the weight of the layers of fabric will pull the pleat down below the skirt hem. This can be corrected by attaching a piece of seam binding or tape to each corner of the top of the pleat and hemming the other end to the waistband.

WAISTS AND WAISTBANDS

Waist finishes suffer a lot of stress and frequently require attention. Also read the sections on *Trousers*, p. 92 and *Skirts*, p. 97, in *Adjustments for Fit and Comfort,* as it may be incorrect fitting that is causing the problem.

Waistband rolls. The quickest solution is to use a length of petersham/grosgrain ¼in (6mm) narrower than the waistband. Place it on back of band, secure with basting tape and topstitch all round band ¼in (6mm), or width of machine foot, from edge, catching edge of stiffening.

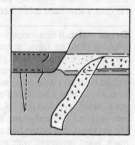

A more time-consuming method is to undo stitching holding waistband to garment leaving 2in (5cm) untouched on each side of the opening. Stitching may be on outside or inside of band; you will have to examine it to find out. You may discover that entire band comes away as you start to unstitch. If this happens, quickly mark across from garment to waistband over seams and darts using fabric marking pen. You can then continue, knowing that you have points to match up again. Open out waistband and look at existing stiffening. If it is wrinkled, press it flat then put a length of Wundaweb/Stitch Witchery underneath and press. This will prevent further wrinkling. Next insert an extra piece of stiffening in waistband. It must be narrower than band itself and not too thick. Use a strip of iron-on interfacing or use Fold-a-Band cut to the necessary width. Place it in position and press. Re-fold waistband and press well. Replace band along top of garment and stitch following old stitching lines and matching any marked points.

Worn or tight waistband. If you want to dispense with the band altogether it can be replaced with a length of curved petersham/grosgrain. Begin by inserting a line of machine stitching around skirt waist beside band. This will prevent stretching. Remove waistband. Fold in upper

edge of skirt along stitching, baste and press. Measure petersham/grosgrain around waist, fold back ends to meet and trim. Hem folded ends and attach a hook and eye, see p. 31, or a piece of Velcro, see p. 36. The petersham/grosgrain must fit the waist comfortably when fastened end to end. Fold petersham/grosgrain in half and mark. Place it inside top of skirt with concave edge just below edge of skirt, place fastening over zipper and match halfway mark to other side of skirt. Secure with basting or basting tape and stitch along edge of petersham/grosgrain. Press.

Waistband too wide. Cut off edge of waistband removing any topstitching, fold in each raw edge evenly and baste. Press each edge then stitch together from end to end close to edge. Remove basting stitches. Stitch again if necessary to imitate other stitching on band. Press.

Dress waist. If belt loops are at wrong level cut them off, snipping close to fabric at base of loop. If new loops are needed make long bar tacks in correct position.

If the only shaping is provided by the belt, the dress should have an elastic stay inside. A belt should not be used to pull in a dress. Use ribbed or open weave elastic cut to fit your waist comfortably plus ¾in (2cm). Make a flat join (see p. 37) and mark the elastic into four sections. Put on dress and fasten belt around. Arrange gathers then mark waist on dress with a row of pins or chalk marks even with lower edge of belt. Take off dress and run a line of basting over pins. Divide waist into four – centre front and back and side seams. Place elastic inside dress with lower edge of waist mark. Attach to dress with zigzag stitch, matching quarters and stretching elastic so that it lies flat on fabric. Remove basting stitches.

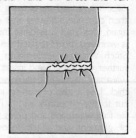

Dress too loose. If attaching an elastic stay to a dress as above is not sufficient, first take in side seams and then insert stay. If dress has a waist seam and an opening, stitch a hook and eye to ends of elastic and attach it to seam allowance, leaving ends loose to fasten under zipper.

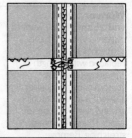

Gaping zipper. If a long dress zipper gapes in wear, sew tapes on each side of zipper, attaching them to seam allowances. Tie them before fastening zipper.

Poor belt. Belts with ready-made dresses sometimes lack style. Simple alternatives can be made using contrasting fabric. For a soft tie belt use a piece of fabric on straight grain 3in (8cm) wide. Fold it RS together, stitch across ends and along the side, leaving a gap in stitching to turn. Trim corners and turn belt RS out by pushing ends through the middle and out of the gap, using a ruler or a knitting needle. Fold remaining edges to meet each other and slipstitch together. Roll belt to bring seam to edge and press.

Other simple belts can be made with a length of fabric tubing. Make this by cutting a narrow strip of fabric on the bias, fold it RS inside and stitch along edge. Turn it RS out using a rouleau needle/ball end bodkin, sewing eye to end of tube and threading it through. Make a knot at each end for a thin belt or thread fabric tubing through a chain or make a plaited belt with three or four pieces.

Another idea is to use a piece of upholstery webbing and fasten it with a pair of leather kilt buckles sewn to the ends.

Belt too short. To lengthen a buckled belt add a piece of fabric of similar weight. Cut fabric twice width of belt plus ¾in (2cm). Fold under ⅜in (1cm) on all edges and press, stitch along each edge to join. Unstitch existing belt overlap to remove buckle. Pass new strip through buckle and around central

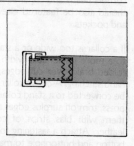

bar. If there is a prong, make an eyelet or attach a metal eyelet. Insert straight end of belt between two ends of strip and stitch twice across width using a wide zigzag stitch.

JACKETS

Buttons. Update a jacket or coat with new buttons of brass, diamanté/rhinestone, horn or whatever fashion suggests. Or cover your own with velvet, suede or braid.

A buttoned jacket can be converted to a Chanel style by removing the collar and cutting off the front edges and attaching folded braid. Apply braid to the cuffs and pockets and, if necessary, shorten the jacket and attach braid around the bottom.

An edge to edge jacket can be given a military look by stitching soutache braid to the edges. Attach two or three pairs of braid frogs and buttons to fasten the jacket at the waist and above.

A riding coat look can be achieved by making a half belt with pointed ends to fasten across the back.

Buttonholes. If loops of bias tubing or cord are not suitable, make buttonholes by machine. Buttonholes in knitted garments can be made as follows: establish position and mark row of knitting. Carefully snip through a stitch at centre and then undo more by pulling end of yarn through. Tie or sew ends securely. Blanketstitch around hole with matching yarn or thread, stitching into each loop of knitting. If several buttonholes are made, hem a piece of soft grosgrain or faille ribbon on the back, cut buttonholes to correspond and buttonhole stitch around them.

See p. 23 for attaching buttons.

Collars. When fashion changes the classic jacket remains the same shape but the collar and lapels on an old one are the giveaway. A narrow collar can be extended by stitching thick braid to the edge. A wider extension can be made by stitching two rows of braid onto a strip of lining. Fold in both edges of lining and press so that it equals width of proposed trimming. Machine or hand stitch trimming then attach to jacket by hemming or slipstitching along one edge. Fold corners neatly and continue along lapel edge. The trimming should also be featured elsewhere, for example, on cuffs and pockets.

If a collar is too wide or a stand collar is too high, reduce it to a more fashionable width by trimming the edge. Apply folded braid over cut edges, attaching it with machine or hand stitching. A classic collar and lapel style can sometimes be converted to a stand collar. Turn collar and lapels up and press, trim off surplus edges and apply folded braid or bind them with bias strips of contrasting fabric or strips of leather. Attach a fastening to top corner of lapel, or add a button and buttonhole to match others on jacket, or fasten with a brooch.

Fur. Strips of fur edging are easy to apply to cuffs and other edges. Hold firmly with edges together and jacket toward you and oversew together. Hem in place along other edge. The pile will conceal stitches. Make joins and corner joins by cutting ends even and oversewing edge to edge. A jacket or coat can be  lengthened by attaching fur strip to extend beyond hem. Cover the back by hemming a wide strip of lining in place with upper edge stitched to coat hem.

Velvet. Sew by hand and make sure pile runs upward on each piece. Cover a collar by pinning a large piece of velvet over it RS up, keeping it in the position it holds when worn. Wrap velvet over collar edges, fold neatly at corners and baste around edge and across back of neck. Trim off surplus leaving ⅜in (1cm). Work herringbone stitch over raw edges. Remove pins and basting. Velvet can be featured elsewhere as pocket flaps. Make up with lining on the back and attach to top of pocket or elsewhere as false flap.

Lining. To replace with new lining, begin by cutting through lining at centre back then carefully remove one half to use as a pattern. Do not undo seam stitching, just cut along stitching to separate pieces. Cut off all hem allowances around edges and cut along dart stitching. Press lining and you have a set of pieces to use as a pattern. Fold new lining in half and pin on old lining, matching straight grain. *Add seam and hem allowances* all round. Place back piece with centre back ¾in (2cm) from fold to allow for pleat for ease. Cut out. Baste pleat in centre back and press. Stitch darts, side and panel seams and press. With jacket WS out, put it over the back of a chair or on a dress form if you have one. Pin lining to jacket, starting at back neck and working in horizontal lines across the back. Make sure you lift the lining high enough for shoulder seams to be joined, but at the same time leave hem allowance at correct level. Pin lining to jacket fronts in the same way with front edges correctly placed to be folded under along jacket facing. Baste lining to jacket securing it first along centre back and seams then stitching 2in (5cm) within all raw edges **(1)**. Join shoulder seams by stitching front seam allowance flat over shoulder then fold under raw edge of back shoulder and baste flat on top. Throughout, remember to keep lining eased onto the jacket; never smooth it flat or it will be tight. Fold under raw edges and baste, easing them back by ¹⁄₁₆in (2mm) as you do so. Baste around hem, front edges and back neck and secure with hemming or slipstitching. Make sleeve linings by stitching and pressing seams, taking a small seam allowance only to ensure that lining has ease. With lining RS out slide it over WS of sleeve. Pull into position at sleeve head, baste lining to sleeve along seam and around cuff and armhole. Fold under raw edge at cuff, ease it back by ¹⁄₁₆in (2mm)

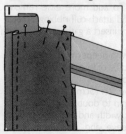
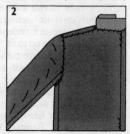

and baste. Fold under ¼in (6mm) seam allowance on sleeve head and baste around armhole. Finish by stitching edges as before **(2)**. Remove all basting and press lining lightly.

Coat loop. Ready-made clothes often lack hanging loops; sometimes the loops they do have break and need replacing. Make a coat loop using a length of firm narrow millinery petersham/grosgrain. Fold under ends and hem very strongly, taking deep stitches into coat fabric at back of neck, not into lining.

A fabric loop can be made by cutting a ¾in (2cm) strip along the selvage of cotton fabric or lining material. Fold over a narrow hem along the long raw edge, fold it twice more, pressing each time. Stitch along each edge of strip securing selvage at the same time. Fold under ends and stitch in position firmly as previously described.

A soft loop for jackets can be made by folding a bias strip of bias binding or lining, stitching and turning RS out using a rouleau needle/ball end bodkin. Attach as before.

SLEEVES

Too long. Almost any style of sleeve can be successfully cut off and re-hemmed at three-quarter, elbow or short length. If a cuffed sleeve is too long, make a series of small pin tucks 2½–3in (6–8cm) above cuff to form a decorative band. Measure accurately from cuff edge to fold and stitch the first tuck, then measure subsequent tucks from the first until sleeve is correct length. Additional decoration such as embroidery or ribbon may be added and the same feature placed elsewhere on the garment.

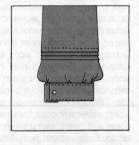

Too short. If sleeves have cuffs, move buttons to the edge to allow cuffs to rise a little. To add more ease remove cuffs, stitch up wrist opening and attach cuff ribbing. Stretch ribbing to fit sleeve. If necessary insert a gathering thread in the sleeve and ease up to fit.

Alternatively, replace cuffs with deeper ones made from a contrasting fabric, or with a ruffle of lace or fabric.

Finally, you could insert bands of contrasting fabric. Draw a line around the sleeve 2in (5cm) below armhole level. Fold sleeve along seam, pin to double fabric with fold even with fold of fabric. Mark width and add ⅝in (1.5cm) seam allowance. Remove sleeve and cut piece to be inserted, making it 2½in (6cm) wider than amount required to lengthen sleeve. Stitch and press seams. Fold in raw edges and press. Cut sleeve, apply band to RS overlapping band onto sleeve, taking ⅝in (1.5cm) seam allowance and matching seams. Topstitch. Add pocket flaps, straps for the shoulders etc., to make contrasting band appear part of a design.

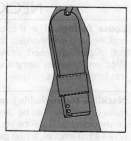

SHOULDERS

Pads. When shoulder pads are in fashion they can be inserted in almost any garment. Have slightly more than half the pad to the front of the shoulder seam and allow it to extend into the armhole by ¼–⅜in (6mm–1cm). Attach to seam allowances at sleeve head with loose oversewing stitches. Unless the garment has a deep armhole you will have to compensate for the pad by re-stitching the underarm curve, lowering it by about ⅜in (1cm). Trim away surplus seam allowance.

Stretched seams. Shoulder seams in knit fabrics and styles with dropped shoulders may stretch after a while. Correct by hemming or machining a piece of seam binding to the shoulder seam, easing fabric onto the tape.

Lingerie straps. Some garments tend to pull lingerie straps off the shoulder. Strap holders can be made by cutting pieces of ribbon 2in (5cm) long, folding in ends and attaching a plastic snap fastener. Fold ribbon and backstitch across the centre to attach it to garment shoulder seam. Place it at least ¾in (2cm) from neck edge so strap and holder will not show. If you have see-through blouses, hide lingerie straps with narrow insertion lace which is a little wider than the straps.

POCKETS

Patch pockets. Reinforce sagging patch pockets by carefully inserting a piece of iron-on interfacing, cut ⅜in (1cm) smaller all round than pocket.

Seam pockets. If seam pockets roll into a ridge, press iron-on interfacing to one side of bag, trimming edge neatly. If pocket bag sags and spoils the line of the garment, attach a piece of tape to top of bag and sew other end to waistband or waist seam.

NECKLINES

Loose facings. The shaped facings on square or low necklines and on sleeveless armholes are inclined to spring out of position. Insert small pieces of Wundaweb/Stitch Witchery between facing and garment and press well so that facing adheres.

Neckline too high. Mark new neckline, taking care not to make it too low. Also be careful not to widen it too much on shoulders or it will be very loose. It is safest to trim off only a small amount, try on garment to check and trim again if necessary. An easy finish for the new neckline is to bind it with bias strips of fabric or ready-made binding. It is not necessary to remove original facings from garment; leave them to support the edge and simply enclose raw edges with binding.

To cut your own bias strips. Draw a line across the fabric at 45 degrees from the selvage. Cut on this line and again several times parallel with it until you have enough. Stitch ends of strips together, in a ¼in (6mm) seam. Press seam open. Pass it through a tape-making tool, pressing the folds as it emerges. The

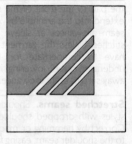

exact width of strip required for the tool will be specified on the pack.

To attach binding. Open out one fold, place on RS of garment with crease on new seamline. There will usually be a seam allowance of ⅝in (1.5cm) on garment which means that edge of binding will be slightly back from edge of garment. This makes it easier to handle as there is a tendency for the bias strip to slip off the

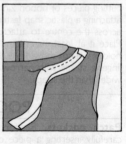

edge. Baste binding in place and stitch. Sew with hand backstitch or machine stitch, following crease in binding. Remove basting, trim raw edge of garment even with binding. With garment RS up, use tip of iron to push binding to extend beyond edge. Fold binding right over edge and baste. Edge of binding should rest on line of stitching. Hem along this edge, taking needle under machine stitches. An alternative finish is to pull binding a little further over and stitch by machine. Sew, RS up, on or just beside binding to catch in the edge beneath. Straight or zigzag stitching may be used.

Binding may also be applied to WS first and finished with machine stitching on RS.

To finish ends of binding, fold under before basting second side and slipstitch across end.

To join ends together, trim strips at an angle of 45 degrees, fold back and press. Place together end to end and slipstitch together. An experienced sewer may prefer to machine stitch ends together.

If the garment already has binding around the neckline it is probably attached with only one line of stitching, and it may be weakened or damaged if you try to remove it which will prevent you from re-using it. The answer is to cut carefully along the line of stitching to detach the binding completely. Replace with a matching or contrasting colour, using commercial prefolded binding or make your own.

New shape neckline. This update is for experienced sewers. A fresh look can be achieved by changing a round neck to a square, V or sweetheart shape. The new edge can be finished with bias binding as described above or shaped facings can be made from spare fabric or lining material.

Put on garment and mark shape you require with pins. Mark around one half of neckline, putting pins within bra edges and shoulder strap positions. Plan to take very little off at shoulder seams. If garment has a back zipper, keep to original neckline as far as shoulder seams rather than having to remove zipper. If garment has a front fastening, new neckline should pass at least ⅝in (1.5cm) above a button.

Take off garment, fold it and pin along centre back and centre front and pin shoulder seams together. Unfasten zipper or buttons. Make sure both layers are together accurately by pushing one sleeve inside the other. Adjust pin line to a good shape. Mark neckline on underside using fabric marking pen and feeling the position of each pin **(1)**. Mark along pinned side and remove pins. Cut around neckline ⅝in (1.5cm) *above* new shape. Remove any remaining facing or neck finish. Place garment, still folded and pinned, on doubled iron-on interfacing. Place garment fold against interfacing fold and outline new neck edge as far as shoulder seam. Mark position of shoulder seams. Remove garment. Complete outline of facing, making it 2in (5cm) wide; rule shoulder seams and add ⅝in (1.5cm) seam allowance. Repeat with back neck **(2**, p. 86**)**.

Cut out, open out pieces and press to WS of fabric. Cut out fabric. Join pieces at shoulder edges, stitching RS together. Press open seams, zigzag outer edge of facing **(3)**. Open out garment, place facing and garment RS together, matching neck edges and shoulder seams and pin. Baste around neckline. It is a good idea to

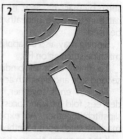

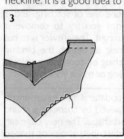

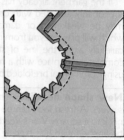

check at this stage by trying on. If you have made the neckline too low, stitch around it with a smaller seam allowance. If by chance it is too high, take a wider seam allowance. Remember that you are checking position of stitching line, not edge.

Stitch around neckline with garment uppermost, taking extra care at top of zipper. Trim and snip seam allowances **(4)**, press by running tip of iron between garment and facing and push facing to extend beyond garment. Roll facing completely to WS and baste along edge. Press. Hold facing in place by folding in ends beside opening and slipstitching, and by herringboning edges of facing where it crosses shoulder seams.

Limp collar or bow. Add crispness to important features by renewing the interfacing. Remove stitching along neckline sufficiently to enable you to insert a strip of iron-on interfacing. Cut interfacing strip to required shape but smaller than area to be stiffened. Smooth it into place, working on the ironing surface, replace collar and insert some pins vertically, stabbing them into the ironing board cover to hold all layers. Press carefully. Re-stitch neck edge and press again.

Neckline too low. If the neckline gapes and is generally ill-fitting, refer to the section on *Necklines* in *Adjustments for Fit and Comfort,* p. 104. However, if you would just like a change of style, add a bias band. You will probably have to use a contrasting fabric so choose an interesting texture;

knits make good edgings. In addition plan to use the fabric elsewhere, perhaps adding similar bands to the sleeves.

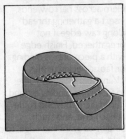

Begin by removing existing neck facing, binding etc. Press edges. Cut new band on the bias, making it twice required width plus 1¼in (3cm). Fold along centre, RS out, and press. Measure band around neckline with raw edges even and pin ends together. Stitch across band, press open, refold fabric. Baste folded band to RS of neckline and stitch. Zigzag along raw edges, press band to extend above neckline.

Detachable features

A plain neckline can be enlivened with a ruffle or cowl. These features will remain in place around the neck without being attached, but if you do want to anchor them use Velcro Spot-Ons/Velcoin fasteners. Space out three or four, stitching the hook pieces to the collar and the loop pieces inside the neck of the garment.

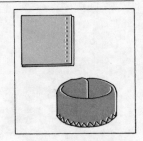

Cowl. Cut a piece of jersey fabric at least 23½in (60cm) long. Fold fabric RS together and join ends. Fold RS out, match raw edges and stitch together. To wear, put it over your head and tuck in the finished edge.

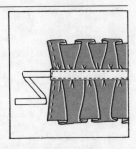

Double ruffle. Use a wide piece of crisp eyeletting or organza, hem all round. Using a piece of ribbon long enough to fit neck comfortably, and ¾in (2cm) wide, gather fabric along centre to fit ribbon. Cover stitching with ribbon and baste, folding in ends. Insert pieces of ribbon for tying into the ends. Stitch all round ribbon to finish. Tie around neck and fold over upper layer.

Single ruffle. Use wide
lace edging or eyeletting.
Hem across narrow ends,
insert a gathering thread
along raw edge if not
pregathered. Finish edge
with a piece of bias binding
or fabric neck size plus
1¼in (3cm). Gather ruffle
to fit, having binding extend
⅝in (1.5cm) beyond ruffle
at each end, and stitch

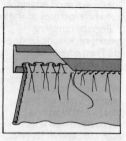

binding to gathered edge, fold in ends ¼in (6mm) onto WS.
Fold binding over gathered edge and stitch. Fasten with a
snap fastener, or leave long ends on the bias fabric to form
tie ends.

ADJUSTMENTS FOR FIT AND COMFORT

When you consider what a variety of shapes and sizes we are it is hardly surprising that ready-made clothes do not always fit to perfection. Men are catered for better than women; the same size suit is usually available with varying sleeve and leg lengths; some jeans are left with unfinished hems to be adjusted before stitching. Women are generally expected to keep looking until they find an outfit that fits, or else alter the size that comes nearest to fitting them.

Comfort in clothes is vital. Poor fit, too big as well as too small, means discomfort. Yet there are many simple, easy-to-make adjustments, even for non-sewers, that will make a garment a better fit and therefore more comfortable. On the other hand, some of the adjustments described in this section necessitate tricky processes such as sewing zippers. If you lack experience or confidence see if you can find someone to help with those parts.

Begin by identifying the problem. Establish exactly where the garment is uncomfortable and then use the following pages to find out why and how to correct it. Remember that darts, tucks, gathers, loose folds of fabric and seams that are curved or shaped all provide the shaping in the fabric that makes the garment fit the body. Often poor or uncomfortable fit is not the result of a garment being too small or too big, but of there being insufficient shape. A dart made wider will produce more shape at its point; fewer gathers will mean less bulk and a closer fit. These and many more small adjustments can make a big difference.

One of the most important things to do after completing an adjustment is to press the garment, especially the area you have altered. This is not difficult as all fabrics respond to heat or heat with moisture, although some may need to be pressed by a dry-cleaner. See *Pressing, Fabrics*, p. 136.

General hints

1. Don't undo too much of the garment. Never let it fall apart completely.

2. When reducing the size make the alteration if possible *before* undoing old stitching; and always cut away surplus fabric afterwards to reduce bulk and improve comfort.

3. Mark the exact extent of the adjustment while wearing the garment. Use pins, tailor's chalk or a fabric marking pen.

4. If you must detach an entire piece, make some matching marks at intervals across the seam before undoing to make it easier to re-join it later.

5. Always check the length of corresponding pairs of darts, seams and so on.

6. Use old stitching holes as a guide.

7. *Never* cut anything off without double checking.

8. Don't overdo it. Remember that adjustments are usually quite small. After all, the garment must almost fit or you would not have bought it in the first place.

BUTTONS

Sometimes simply moving buttons is all that is needed. Buttons can usually be moved up to ⅜in (1cm) either way without upsetting any nearby feature such as a collar or zipper. If a button-through garment such as a shirt fits at one end of the opening but not the other, move just some of the buttons, sewing them in a sloping line. If one button constantly comes undone yet the garment is loose, replace with a larger button.

If several buttons pop open on a blouse or dress, shorten the buttonholes. Oversew or make a simple bar tack inside the round end, or keyhole, which is nearest the garment edge so that the stitches will be concealed when the button is fastened.

If the opening is too tight, for example on a shirt, make an extension by cutting a piece of grosgrain ribbon or cotton tape, hemming each end and placing it beneath the underlap of the garment. Topstitch to hold. Move the buttons over to the extension.

Tight cuffs are as uncomfortable as loose ones and it takes just a few moments to move the buttons.

See p. 23 for attaching buttons.

HEMS

Skirts and trousers which are too short or too long might spoil an otherwise well-fitting and attractive outfit. To lengthen substantially you may have to add a false hem or band of new fabric, see *Extension hem*, p. 47, and *Skirt too short*, p. 74, but there is a chance that the cause is tightness somewhere and that letting it out will lengthen the garment sufficiently. Read the following pages to find out what can be done.

If a plain garment is too long at the hemline or if you have enough hem to let down there will be no problem. Just mark it all around parallel with the floor, press out the old folds, turn it up and make a new hem. See *Trousers*, p. 71, and *Skirts*, p. 72.

Pleated hems

These are less simple to alter but the results depend as much on good pressing as on careful sewing. A compromise solution, which will reduce total working time, is to do the sewing yourself and then take the garment to the dry-cleaners to be pressed.

Flat pleats. If pleat seams were stitched after sections of hem were turned up it means more work in altering the length. Remove stitching in each pleat seam to above hem edge if you are lengthening, or to three times hem depth if you are shortening. Undo stitching all round hem and press so that all pieces hang freely. Insert a pin at level of new length required. Use a hem marker, see *Uneven hem*, p. 73, and measure evenly from floor to level of pin, marking with pins or chalk, or measure evenly from waist with skirt folded along centre back and arranged flat on the table. Fold up each section of skirt with pins and baste close to fold (**1**). Pin each pleat seam together, checking carefully on both sides that hem edges are even when pleat is folded into position (**2**). Adjust and baste again if necessary. Remove pins. Trim off any surplus fabric, leaving 1¼-2in (3-5cm) to turn up. There will, of course, be less if you are lengthening the skirt. Finish raw edge with zigzag or oversewing. Press fold but not stitched edge.

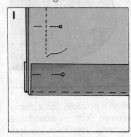
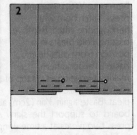

Baste along each pleat seam through hem and along seam as far as end of original stitching. Machine stitch each seam and remove basting. Finish hem with hand catch stitch, blind hemming, or Wundaweb/ Stitch Witchery. Finish edges across the hem with oversewing to prevent fraying ends from hanging

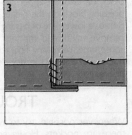

below hemline (**3**). Fold pleats into position on RS of garment, baste to hold and press to finish.

Permanent pleating. Hems have to be narrow so it is impossible to lengthen permanent pleating. Before shortening permanent pleating from the hem, see *Skirts*, p. 97, because it could be that the whole garment needs lifting. However, contrary to popular belief, permanent pleating can be cut off at the hem and re-hemmed. Narrow pleats and sunray pleating in synthetic fabrics are made permanent using heat and moisture until the yarns crack, forming a fold. Experienced sewers will know how to apply more heat using the iron and a damp cloth to make new pleats after hemming, but your dry-cleaner will do it if you are unsure of your skill with the iron. If your pleated skirt is wool, the application of heat and moisture will remove old pleats and also put in new ones. Absolutely permanent pleats can only be made in synthetics because natural yarns do not crack. Even though the hem is machine stitched originally, results are best if the alteration is hand sewn, as this keeps the hem more receptive to being pressed back into pleats.

Mark new length evenly all round. Allow ⅜–⅝in (1–1.5cm) to turn up and cut off surplus. Press edge flat; in wool this will remove pleat lines completely.

Oversew raw edge by hand or, if you are quite sure it will not fray, trim it with pinking shears. Fold up hem onto WS, baste and press. Stitch hem with herringbone stitch. Remove basting. Fold pleats into position from outside and baste all around hem, making two stitches on top of each other through each 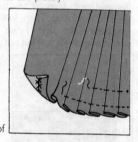 pleat. Baste again ¾in (2cm) above. If possible, use a sleeve board to support the skirt. Arrange skirt on board and press two pleats at a time using a damp cloth. Remove cloth quickly and bang in the steam with a pounding or pressing block or tailor's clapper. Allow to cool with pounding or pressing block on the pleats. Press like this all around skirt. Remove lower line of basting and press again more lightly to remove any thread imprints. Hang the skirt by the waist for some time, removing final row of basting after a couple of hours. Take it to the dry-cleaners to be pressed again if necessary.

TROUSERS

Whenever possible, try to avoid making alterations where there are pockets. However, if this is unavoidable, patch pockets will have to be removed and replaced later; bag seam pockets as found on women's clothes can be re-stitched; inset angled pockets such as on men's trousers should be left unaffected by alterations. Alternatively, remove pockets completely and stitch up the seam. Trousers tend to get hard wear; so it is a good idea to make two rows of stitching for strength, one on top of the other. Although machine stitching is stronger, it is often very difficult to manipulate the trousers so that you can reach the area. Hand backstitch is a good substitute. See p. 71 for methods of dealing with hems.

See also *Sewing for Children*, p. 120.

Waist too big – women's and children's trousers.

A small reduction in size can be made by inserting elastic through the waistband. Use firm non-roll elastic slightly narrower than the waistband to fit across the back or, for a larger alteration, to extend across the back and round to the front almost to darts.

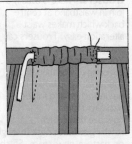

On inside of band, carefully cut two vertical slits through one layer of fabric. On woven fabrics oversew edges to prevent fraying. Pin one end of elastic to waistband, thread other end through band and bring it out of other slit. Secure one end by stitching twice across band through all layers. Pull up elastic to make necessary reduction and stitch across other end in the same way. Trim ends and tuck into slits out of sight.

A smoother line, and more shaping for your bottom, is produced by the following method; this is an alteration not generally required on children's trousers, but it could be used if the previous alteration is unsuitable.

Calculate total reduction in waist size needed and divide by four. Remove waistband across back of trousers to enable you to reach darts. Cut through waistband at centre back. Re-stitch centre back seam taking ¼ of your total reduction at the waist (remember this fabric is double). Slope stitching gradually until it re-joins original stitching just above crotch curve. Remove original stitching up to waist. Press seam open. Trim edges if necessary. Re-stitch darts taking ¼ of your total reduction on each at waist and making them about ⅜in (1cm) longer than original darts **(1)**. Press. Re-join ends of waistband, opening out fabric and stitching across. Band must fit new waist edge exactly.

If you find it difficult to join band accurately, fold in and press ends so that they meet and slipstitch together by hand from RS **(2)**. Replace band on trousers and stitch. Press.

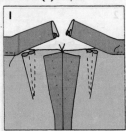

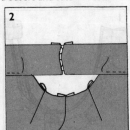

Waist too big – men's trousers. There is usually a join in waistband at centre back which makes waist alteration easy. Trousers can also be let out at this point. You will probably find a covering of waistbanding or rubberized grip which must be unstitched and folded back. You can now see that crotch

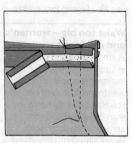

stitching extends right through outer piece of waistband. Pin or baste a new seam. Stitch from waistband in a smooth line, re-joining old stitching above crotch curve. Remove old stitching, trim seam if necessary and press open. Hem seam allowances to upper edge of band. Replace waistband covering and hem in place with ends folded under to meet in a seam on top of waistband seam.

Baggy under the bottom. This seems to be a more common problem with women's trousers. The solution is to lift the excess fabric into the crotch seam.

Remove waistband for 4in (10cm) or so each side of centre back seam. On inside of trousers mark a new stitching line to dip down in a more exaggerated curve from inside leg seam. Make sure line re-joins original seam smoothly. Begin new curve at about hip level on the back, dipping it by ⅜in (1cm) or more at the point marked with an arrow on the illustration **(1)**. Do not take too much off inside leg seam or you will create a new problem. Re-join old seam below zipper. Stitch new seam, trim off surplus fabric and try on the trousers. You can now lift them higher at the back waist which helps eliminate bagginess. If trousers are still baggy below the bottom, stitch again taking another ¼in (6mm) at position shown by arrow. Press open top part of seam and replace waistband, pinning it with surplus fabric pulled up above it **(2)**. When lifting trousers higher at the back in this way, make sure you do not make them too short in the leg length. Trim off surplus at waist and stitch waistband in place.

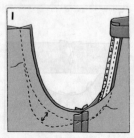

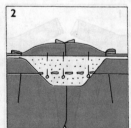

Crotch too high. The simplest way of relieving a tight crotch is to loosen the waist fastening to lower the trousers. If this doesn't work see whether the seams can be re-stitched. This is difficult on jeans which have welt seams and is probably not worth attempting. Some trousers and jeans have the inside leg seams stitched in one run after each part of the crotch seam has been joined. You cannot lower the crotch on these (although raising it is very simple – just re-stitch the inside leg seam). Trousers that have both seam allowances on the inside can easily have the crotch lowered.

With trousers inside out and one leg tucked inside the other, mark a new crotch seamline to cross inside leg seams ⅜in (1cm) below existing stitching. From this point, curve the line straight up to back seam. On the front continue the new lower line and then curve it up to meet original stitching.

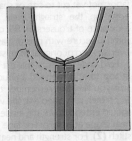

Keep new line directly below old one; do not extend to right or left beyond it or you will widen the crotch curve and the legs will be stitched closer together giving an impossible fit. Trim seam allowances.

Low crotch. This adjustment should not be attempted by beginners. Note that raising the crotch will shorten the legs, and if the hems cannot be let down it may not be worth making the alteration. The adjustment cannot be made to trousers with a side zipper unless you are prepared to take it out and replace it later.

Decide how much to lift trousers. Remove waistband except for ¾-1¼in (2-3cm) at top of zipper.

Mark a new waistline below old stitching line, curving it very gradually up to meet old line near zipper. Measure length of old darts and their width at old waistline and mark and stitch new darts the same size and length from new waistline. Measure the distance between darts and seams at old waistline.

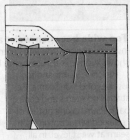

Repeat these measurements from new darts on new waistline and mark new seamlines. You can see that if you did not do this the waist would be much too big. Stitch new seams. Press darts. Remove original stitching from seams and press open. Replace waistband following new waistline. Stitch, trim off surplus fabric and finish.

Waistband too high. This indicates that the trousers are too long between waist and crotch. The adjustment required is the same as described under *Low crotch* but note that in this case you may be compelled to remove the zipper and lower the waistline by an even amount all round.

Tight around thighs. This adjustment involves inserting a triangular gusset of additional, similar fabric.

Undo 2in (5cm) of crotch seam stitching and sufficient stitching along each inside leg seam. Take a piece of new fabric not yet cut to size or shape, fold under and press one edge on the straight grain. Place this on front seam allowance of trousers on RS, overlapping raw edge by ¼in (6mm). Secure with pins or basting tape and stitch so that it overlaps end of original seam stitching by ¾in (2cm) **(1)**.

Fold under fabric to make a triangle which is wide enough at top to add required amount. You can make gusset any size you like, but remember that it increases the width of the crotch curve and that the wider the gusset the further it should extend down the inside leg seam. Press fold, make a neat shape at base, pin or tape to edge of back leg seam and stitch **(2)**. For strength and neatness sew along both sides of gusset. Pin crotch seam edges RS together, matching gusset seams, and mark a curved stitching line. Stitch seam, overlapping ends of original stitching for strength. Trim surplus fabric at top of gusset and finish edges.

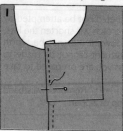
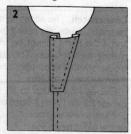

Too wide between waist and crotch. This adjustment involves altering side and centre back seams. The illustration shows women's trousers with bag seam pockets.

Remove waistband to just beyond side seams. Re-stitch side seams and centre back seam, taking out ⅓ of required reduction in each seam at waist level. In all three cases, the new seam must slope gently to meet original seam 1 ¼in (3cm) above crotch level to avoid bulges. Remove old stitching. Trim and press

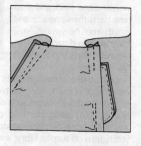

seams. To ensure that pocket lies flat, cut off edge of pocket bag (instead of undoing stitching) and separate the two pieces. Press seams and pocket flat. Pin bag pieces together and re-stitch around outer edge. Trim off surplus fabric. Cut waistband across at centre back. Join ends to fit new waistline and attach to top of trousers.

Loose at inside leg and crotch. This is an easy adjustment except on jeans with double-stitched seams.

Undo a short piece of crotch seam. Re-stitch inside leg seams taking a little off the top and sloping new stitching to meet original seam 6-8in (15-20cm) below. Remove old stitching, press seams. Pin crotch seam together, matching seams, and re-stitch.

SKIRTS

Skirt adjustments are, on the whole, not difficult. Save yourself work by trying to alter seams other than the one with the zipper in it. Apart from the way a skirt feels, you can often detect problems by looking at it from the side. The side seam should hang at right angles to the floor. If it swings to the back it indicates that the front is too long and needs lifting. If the seam swings to the front, the back may need lifting unless seating is the problem. Sometimes the excess length shows as a horizontal fold of fabric below the waist at the back or front.

Consult the *Skirts* section in *Renovations and Improvements*, p. 72, for instructions on straightening hems, shortening and lengthening.

Baggy under the bottom. If this is not caused by seating (see *Skirts that seat*, p. 67) it means that the skirt is too long at the back in relation to the front. The excess has to be lifted into the waist seam. It is not a difficult adjustment but if the skirt has a back zipper you must be confident that you can remove it and put it back again.

With the skirt on, pinch out and pin a horizontal fold of fabric below waist at back. Take off the skirt and measure depth of fold at centre back. Remove pins, mark a new back waistline from base of waistband at side seams, curving down at centre back to depth required. Remove waistband across the back and zipper if necessary. Re-stitch darts making them wider and longer: measuring from new waistline, make them the same size as they were originally. Press darts. Replace zipper if appropriate, opening the seam further and placing slider below new waist seam. Replace waistband, attaching it to new waist marking. Trim off surplus edge of skirt and complete waistband stitching.

Wrinkles below back waist. The cause and the solution are the same as above. Follow instructions for lifting excess fabric into the waist seam.

Wrinkles below front waist. This indicates that the front is too long in relation to the back, although if the hem rises at the front it is more likely that the skirt is a bit tight across the stomach. If this seems to be the case, follow instructions on facing page for this type of problem.

Decide how much needs to be removed by pinning a fold of fabric across front. Mark a new waistline starting at side seams and curving down at centre front. Remove waistband across front. If you have a very flat stomach, re-stitch the darts making them longer and wider, but most people will achieve a better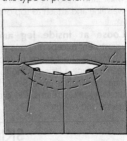

and more comfortable fit by using smaller darts or tucks. Replace waistband on new line, easing in slight extra fullness from edge of skirt. Trim off excess fabric and finish.

Wrinkles below waist all round. To make this adjustment the zipper must be removed. If the skirt is the correct length but there is surplus fabric below the waist, or if the waist rises up too high on the body, it indicates that the skirt is too long between the waist and hip levels.

Fold out and pin necessary amount. Note that amount you remove need not necessarily be equal all round – see the three previous adjustments. Mark a new waistline around skirt. Remove waistband and zipper. Re-stitch upper part of side seams, taking them in a little at new waist level.

Re-stitch all darts making them wider but not longer – the short figure will be better fitted with shorter darts. Replace zipper and waistband, checking the size against new waist.

Tight across thighs. A shaped or A-line skirt can be lifted at the waist to loosen it at thigh level as described above under *Wrinkles below waist all round*. A straight skirt must be let out.

Undo hem at side seams and mark new stitching lines on side seams beginning at hip level and curving out over thighs. Continue lines straight to hem, letting out as much as possible. Stitch seams. Undo old stitching and press. If there are only very small seam allowances left, press both toward back of skirt and topstitch from RS parallel with seamline. Replace hem and press.

Tight across stomach. There are two possible solutions to this problem. In severe cases both adjustments will have to be made.

Remove enough of the waistband to be able to reach darts. Remove all dart stitching and press fabric flat. Make four small folds to form tucks, two on each side, near position of old darts **(1)**. Replace waistband.

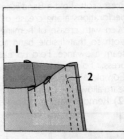

The second adjustment is easy to make on skirts with a back zipper. Remove waistband on both sides above side seams. Keeping waist size the same, re-stitch side seams curving out from waistline to hip level **(2)**. Undo old stitching. Press seams. Replace waistband.

Front hem rises. This may happen because the skirt is tight across the stomach and surplus fabric rises above the waistline. In this case follow instructions above.

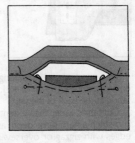

Remove waistband and mark new curved line above old stitching line running from sides up to centre of skirt. If there is insufficient seam allowance, extend it first by stitching a piece of tape or seam binding to edge. Re-stitch darts making them shorter, or even remove altogether and put in small tucks, which is a more comfortable solution. Replace waistband, attaching it to new higher waistline.

Waist too tight. Front darts can be made smaller or removed altogether, which will provide an additional ¾in (2cm) or more at the waist. Side seams can be let out above hip level, unless there is a side zipper. The centre back seam can also be let out if there is no zipper.

Remove waistband except for final 2in (5cm) or so where the buttonhole is. Re-stitch seams and front darts to let out as described. Press skirt. Baste waistband back in position. Remove button and extend waistband sufficiently to fit the skirt by attaching a double piece of similar fabric. Stitch and finish waistband. Attach button.

A more comfortable alternative is to discard the waistband altogether and replace it with petersham/grosgrain, pre-curved for preference, or attach non-roll elastic of the type used on the tops of knitted skirts.

Too tight to walk. Straight skirts are sometimes very narrow at the hem, especially if they are long with plain open seams. Make a slit at one or both side seams to provide walking space.

Mark a suitable depth of slit on seams. Unstitch hemline at that point. On inside of skirt undo seam stitching to required depth. Re-stitch ¾-1¼in (2-3cm) to reinforce it. Press soft Fold-a-Band/Fuse-n-Fold to seams, lining up perforations along crease of stitched seam **(1)**. Trim end even with crease of hemline. Press with iron over damp cloth so that fusible band adheres. Trim edge even with seam allowance. Fold up each corner of hem, baste and press. Fold back seam allowances, baste and press. Complete hem stitching and oversew to secure edge of seam allowance to hem. Make a simple bar tack at top of slit **(2)**. Remove basting and press from RS.

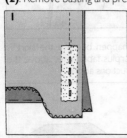
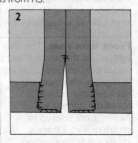

If you need to make a long slit at the hem it can be converted into a Dior or kick pleat by hanging a piece of fabric at the back of the slit.

Cut fabric wider than extent of seam allowances. Turn up and stitch a hem same depth as garment. Finish other three edges with zigzag or oversewing. Place the piece RS down on inside of skirt with hems even. Attach upper edge to seam above top of slit with herringbone stitch.

Skirt too big. If the skirt has a back zipper the side seams can be taken in as described, but if the alteration involves removing the zipper and waistband completely it should only be attempted by the experienced sewer.

Remove waistband at each side above seams. Cut through waistband above each seam. Put skirt on inside out and pin new, tighter, side seams. If you can pin a seam that slopes out to meet the old seam above the hem, it will save a lot of work. If it is essential to reduce the width of the skirt right through the

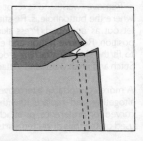

hemline, you will have to undo enough of the hem to enable you to pin right to the bottom. Take skirt off, baste along new seamline, remove pins. Straighten seamline below hip level by drawing a straight line using tailor's chalk and a ruler. Stitch new seams, sewing from bottom up to waist. If alteration is substantial trim off excess fabric evenly, leaving ⅝in (1.5cm) seam allowance. Undo any old stitching left beside new seam. Press seams. Join ends of waistband with band opened out and RS together. Stitch across band taking a seam allowance equal to the amount by which you reduced the side seam. Press open seams. Replace waistband on skirt. Stitch and press. Re-stitch hem if you have had to undo it.

Gathered skirt too full.
If a gathered skirt feels too bulky and full, try moving some of the gathers.

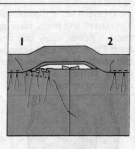

Unstitch waistband at side seams and around front but leave it attached at centre front. Remove gathering thread, press skirt edge flat. Insert a new gathering thread with running stitches or a line of large straight machine stitching along front of skirt, stopping 2in (5cm) from side seam **(1)**. Pull up gathers. Pin waistband to skirt, keeping skirt flat over side seam and arranging gathers along front of skirt. Baste and stitch waistband.

The alternative is to fold the skirt into several unpressed pleats instead of gathers **(2)**. If neither of these remedies is sufficient to cure the bagginess, undo the hem at the sides and reduce fullness by stitching new side seams, taking in as much as necessary. Trim and finish seams, attach waistband and turn up hem.

Back seam stands out. Undo hem at back. Baste a new seamline from just above hip level to hem, sloping it gradually to take in surplus. Stitch new seam, remove old stitching and press. Re-stitch hem.

Panel skirt too loose. If a skirt with several seams is generally loose or too full all round, divide up the fullness and take in each seam by a small amount. This will keep the line of the skirt better than taking in side seams only.

If the panels are flared at the hem, giving a fishtail effect, the full flare can be retained by stitching in a smooth curve from below thigh level.

If the flare is formed by triangular inserts you will have to undo the stitching at the top of each insert, re-stitch the seams, then re-stitch the inserts.

BODICES

Smaller amounts of fabric are involved but they are possibly trickier alterations because usually more than one seam has to be undone. However, it is usually worth the trouble because an ill-fitting bodice can cause great discomfort.

Tight below armholes. A simple remedy is to remove stitching in back waist darts, leaving tucks **(1)**.

If more ease is required see whether garment is suitable for letting out by making an insertion at centre front from neck to hem. The insertion can be contrasting fabric, braid or even an open-ended zipper **(2)**. Fold garment carefully to find centre front and press to make a crease. Cut along the crease. If fabric is to be inserted, fold in garment edges ¼in (6mm) and press, place on RS of insert and stitch. To insert a zipper, apply bias binding to garment edges and finish. Place outer edge of binding beside zipper teeth, baste and stitch. In both cases make matching marks before cutting garment and then make certain edges are even when lining up insert.

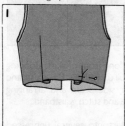
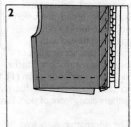

Bodice too loose. If garment fits above armhole level but is too loose below, make a simple reduction by sloping the side seam. Take out necessary amount at waist or hemline and taper it to nothing beside armhole.

SHOULDERS

Tight across shoulder blades. Re-stitch back armhole seam from shoulder to curve of underarm. Let out seam as much as possible, placing a piece of seam binding or tape underneath to reinforce it and prevent splitting later. If garment has a centre back seam let that out too between neckline and armhole level.

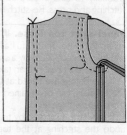

Remove all old stitching on seams and press. If garment has

long sleeves and buttoned cuffs it helps to move buttons to loosen cuffs.

Too wide. Experienced sewers will be able to remove top of sleeve and mark a new line on bodice, making shoulders narrower, and then replace sleeve head. Others will find the following solution much easier. Make two tucks by pinning folds of fabric on outside of garment to lift armhole seam up onto  shoulder. Baste and press tucks and stitch. If garment is big all over, tucks can be stitched right through to hem. Otherwise end stitching at a point halfway down armhole at back and front.

Too square. This is evident from loose diagonal folds that run from the neck area to the armhole. It is tedious to remove the sleeves and re-stitch the shoulder seams because width of sleeve must also be reduced to fit. An easier solution is to insert shoulder pads to fill out the surplus.

ARMHOLES

Too low. If the armhole is too low and the garment looks baggy and shapeless a neater fit can be achieved by taking in the side seams. If garment is loose all over, continue new stitching line down to hem. If not, run new stitching into original line at waist level. Stitch new side seam and sleeve seam, running stitching into 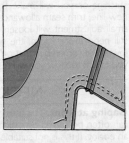 original seam at elbow level. Trim and snip seam allowance. Take care not to reduce size too much or movement will be restricted, especially if garment has a dropped shoulder line.

If the armhole of a fitted garment is too low it can only be remedied by raising the shoulders. This is a complicated adjustment that should only be attempted by experienced sewers and only then if the garment is worth it. The adjustment also raises the waistline and bust darts, so check by pinning the shoulders to make sure the new length will be satisfactory.

Remove sleeves and sufficient neck facing to enable you to reach shoulders. Lift shoulders and re-stitch seam. If raising armhole by up to ⅜in (1 cm), slope stitching to blend with old seam at neck edge. Trim, press open. If sleeve has a smooth plain head, re-stitch sleeve seam to reduce width to

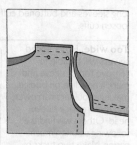

correspond with reduction in armhole size. Note that sleeves in knits and soft fabrics can usually be eased into the new armhole.

Too high. Try removing shoulder pads if there are any. If that does not solve the problem, mark a new stitching line to cross underarm and bodice seams ¼in (6mm) below existing stitching. Curve it up to re-join original armhole stitching. Make sure you only lower the base of the armhole; do not

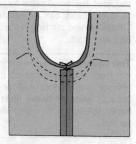

extend the line outwards to right or left beyond original stitching or you will make the garment smaller. Stitch on new line, trim seam allowance and oversew raw edge. This small adjustment will loosen armhole considerably. If you still need more room, the new line can be taken a little lower but remember that on a dress or a fitted garment if you take it too low you will restrict arm movement.

NECKLINES

Gaping at front. This usually occurs on low necklines and can often be solved by making a separate insert or adding an edging. If this is not suitable a more extensive adjustment can be made in one of the following ways.

Begin by removing neckline finish to beyond shoulder seams. Fold surplus at neckline into several tucks, baste in place then stitch to prevent neckline stretching **(1)**.

If tucks are not suitable or if there is only a small amount of surplus in neck edge, insert a gathering thread and pull up, arranging gathers evenly **(2)**.

If the garment is close fitting, or the fabric crisp, make two short darts, one on each side of the centre front, angled towards the bust **(3)**.

The final possibility is to lift and re-stitch shoulder seams **(4)**. Slope stitching from new point at neck to join original

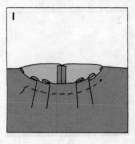 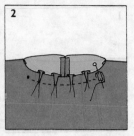

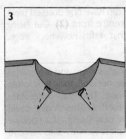 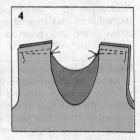

seam before reaching armhole. Remove old stitching, press seams.

After reducing neck edge in one of these ways, cut neck facing in the centre and re-join so that it fits new neckline. Replace facing and press to finish.

Loose back neck. If a garment stands away from the neck, remove facing to beyond shoulder seams. Pin and stitch two small darts, one each side of centre back. Press and replace neck facing, folding surplus under at zipper. If there is a centre back seam, re-join ends of facing so that facing fits new smaller neck edge.

Neck too wide. A square or boat-shaped neckline may be too wide, causing sleeveless garments to fall off the shoulders. It is usually sufficient to reduce the width of the front neckline only and this can be done decoratively.

Remove neck facing on front. Mark centre of bodice by creasing with the iron. Stitch two or three vertical tucks from neck (**1**, p. 106). If bodice is loose enough, tucks can be stitched right to the waist. If not, make them short and stitch them on the outside. With a square neck, make one tuck at each corner.

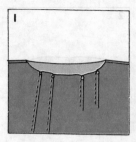

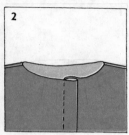

Alternatively, either neck shape can have one pressed pleat stitched from neck to waist at centre front **(2)**. Cut facing across centre and re-join so that it fits new neck edge. Attach, stitch, finish and press.

Neck too high. This is an easy adjustment and it provides an opportunity to re-shape the neckline too. It is often sufficient to lower only the front. This may necessitate finishing the neck by a different method. Bias binding could be used or contrasting fabric for new facings. If a neckline with a collar is too high, the simplest remedy is to remove the collar.

Mark the new neckline as required. An adjustment of 1¼in (3cm) or less can easily be made on a collarless neckline. Bring neck facing over onto RS and pin flat. Stitch along marked line on garment and through facing, running stitching smoothly into original line at shoulders **(1)**. Trim off surplus to within

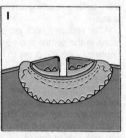

⅜in (1cm) of new stitching. Snip seam allowances. Roll facing to WS. Press.

If neckline is to be lowered more than this or perhaps re-shaped, remove front facing as far as each shoulder seam and detach along facing seams. Baste bias binding, opened

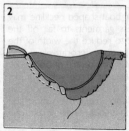

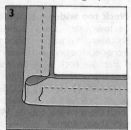

out flat, to RS of garment, matching crease to new marked neckline. Allow binding ends to overlap back facing by ⅝in (1.5cm). Stitch binding to neckline. Snip raw edges, roll binding completely to inside of neck; baste along edge making sure binding will not show from RS. Slipstitch or hem outer edge of binding to garment, taking care not to allow stitches to show through to RS. Tuck ends of binding under back neck facing and hem to shoulder seams **(2)**.

If new neckline is square, V or heart-shaped, fold binding neatly at corners when attaching it so that it lies flat when folded over the edge **(3)**.

Front neck rises. If the neckline seems to get higher while you wear the garment it indicates that the front is too long (or the back is too short, but there is no remedy for that except in loose one-piece clothes). If you think that the neckline is too high, lower it by following the instructions for *Neck too high* on facing page, but the real problem may be the length of the bodice.

Pin out a tuck across garment above waist to bring down neckline and also to shape the bust – which may be the cause of the problem. Stitch following the pins. The tuck runs to nothing at the side seams. The alternative, for experienced sewers only, is to undo waist seam and cut off surplus before re-stitching.

SLEEVES

Cuffs with buttons can be adjusted by moving the buttons, either to loosen or to tighten. Other adjustments to length can be found in the section on *Sleeves* in *Renovations and Improvements*, p. 82. There is a limit to further alteration due to the shape of a sleeve, but in some cases an uncomfortable fit can be alleviated even if it cannot be entirely corrected.

Top too tight. If the sleeve is too tight around the upper arm, insert a gusset of similar fabric in the sleeve and bodice. Quite a small piece will usually suffice but if contrasting fabric has to be used it may look better to use larger pieces and also to use the contrast elsewhere on the garment.

Open bodice and sleeve seams from underarm for required length. Press. Fold in and press one edge of two pieces of contrast, apply to RS of garment, placing fold on top of one seam edge. Baste in position. Fold under the end

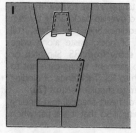

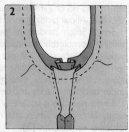

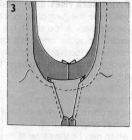

and second edge to form a triangle **(1)**. Make sure both gussets are the same width, although they can vary in length. Stitch in place close to edge. With sleeve and bodice RS together, re-stitch armhole, curving stitching as it crosses gussets **(2)**. Trim off surplus fabric and oversew edges. The shape of the gussets as they appear on the outside can be varied, provided the amount inserted is a small triangle.

If armhole is too high on original garment, insert a sleeve gusset and lower armhole on bodice to compensate when replacing sleeve **(3)**.

Loose raglan or kimono sleeve. This is common on people with narrow or sloping shoulders. The solution with both types of sleeve is to take in the seam running from neck to wrist **(1)**. Raglan styles often do not have this seam so simply pin out the necessary amount on WS and stitch in a smooth curve from near the neckline over the shoulder to the elbow or below **(2)**.

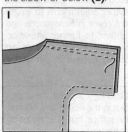

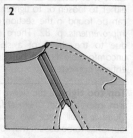

These adjustments put more shape into the sleeve and they can make loose fitting designs more flattering. Alternatively, the surplus could be stitched along the outside of the sleeve in one or more tucks.

Loose at wrist. A small reduction can be made by re-stitching the sleeve seam from the wrist for a distance of 4-5in (10-12cm). If more than ⅜in (1cm) or so is removed you run the risk of restricting elbow movement. Any more surplus should be taken out in a dart at the wrist made further round toward the little finger.

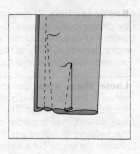

Tight fitted sleeve. If a long fitted sleeve feels uncomfortable, check the position of the elbow dart. If it is not at your elbow level it is worth moving it. Undo part of the sleeve seam, undo the dart and move it to a new position, making it shorter than the original for greater comfort. Re-stitch sleeve seam.

DRESSES

Some of the adjustments already described apply to dresses; more specific alterations are set out below, but remember to check the fit of the entire garment.

Waisted dress rises. Loosen the waist by lengthening or removing the elastic or letting out the bodice and skirt side seams a little. If this is not possible you may be able to lengthen the bodice by dropping it at the shoulder seams. This might be worth doing on a sleeveless, collarless style dress. If the bodice is fitted with darts, the rising waistline may be the result of the underarm dart being too high. The direction of darts should be toward the bust point or slightly below. If the waist is too high it means the bust is taking the shape it requires from below.

Unstitch bust dart and re-pin in correct direction. It may be possible to do this without disturbing the side seams, but if not, unstitch for a short distance remove darts and re-stitch with points lower. Re-stitch seams.

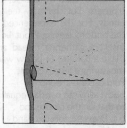

Tight across bust. Check direction of bust darts as explained above and lower them if necessary. When re-stitching, make them shorter than they were originally to provide more room. When re-stitching side seams let them out as much as possible.

Bodice too long. Remove surplus length above the waist by pinning out a tuck on RS midway between waist and underarm. Stitch the surplus as a tuck and press flat. For a more decorative finish, divide up the amount to be taken out and make several small tucks.

Loose chest area. Sometimes surplus fabric appears between the neckline and bust level. This excess also makes the front neckline loose. This can be removed in a vertical tuck down the centre front or in a horizontal tuck below the neckline. In both cases the tuck runs to nothing as it reaches the seams, but a vertical tuck must be taken into the neckline, so begin by removing the neck facing. Stitch tuck on RS and press. When replacing a neck facing make a seam at the centre to ensure facing fits new neckline.

One-piece dress. This may appear baggy under the bottom but you can remedy this by lifting the dress at shoulder level. If there is no back zipper, make a horizontal tuck below the neckline as decribed above for *Loose chest area*. (The alternative method involves removing the sleeves and neckline finish and should be attempted by experienced sewers only.)

Undo the shoulder seams and raise the back only. Re-stitch and press. The sleeve now has to be reduced to fit the new armhole. Re-stitch the sleeve seam, taking out the same amount as the adjustment at the shoulder. Replace the sleeves. Reduce the length of the neck facing by re-stitching the shoulder seams, then replace the neck facing.

Skirts of dresses can be adjusted as explained earlier under *Skirts*, p. 97. Side slits can also be added to straight dresses.

BLOUSES

Blouse rides up. Shirts and blouses that often come untucked can, of course, be worn outside a skirt or trousers, but this may feel uncomfortably loose or look untidy. For the experienced sewer, a solution is to cut off the bottom, leaving about 4in (10cm) below the waistline. Insert a gathering thread around lower edge of blouse. Make a band to fit below waist on top of your hip bone by measuring a length of soft Fold-a-Band around the body; allow an overlap equal to that on the blouse and cut. Press perforated band to WS of surplus fabric, matching perforations to the straight grain. Cut out around band, adding a seam allowance. Fold strip RS together and

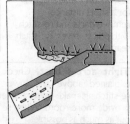

stitch across ends. Turn RS out, fold in edges and press. Pull up gathers to fit band, slip edge of blouse between edges of band. Baste and stitch. Fasten ends of band with a hook or Spot-On/Velcoin fastener.

Blouse tight over hips. Shortening the blouse and marking a new hem may solve this problem but an equally easy solution is to make side slits as described in *Skirts*, p. 100. Alternatively, cut the lower edge to shirt-tail shape and make a new hem.

SEWING FOR CHILDREN

For many people their first introduction to sewing is by way of children's clothes. This is a wonderful way of learning to sew. It is quicker and less demanding than making adult clothes, because the pieces are smaller and the processes are simpler; you might need only four buttons instead of eight for example. In addition, quick techniques and short cuts can often be used and you will be less nervous of things going wrong. The child will not mind that you are feeling your way and experimenting.

Odd pieces can be combined and remnants and good fabric from old garments can be used, so the outlay is often quite small. You may be able to reduce it still more by using buttons, zippers and fasteners you already have. Provided that the results are comfortable and fashionable the child will probably be quite happy.

Baby clothes are less easy because they are fiddly; nevertheless, beginners can learn basic stitches and techniques on simply-styled garments.

Although some of the information in other sections of this book is applicable, children's clothes have special requirements, mainly because children are constantly active and growing.

General hints

If you are new to sewing for children the following tips and suggestions may be of help.

1. Don't economize on sewing equipment; these tasks are so much less of a chore if you have the right tools and many of the modern aids available make it fun.

2. Do have the iron set up. This is not only for pressing each complete stage; also, it is so much quicker to fold and press an edge than to baste, fold and press, and then still have the basting to remove.

3. Keep the paper pattern for future use, putting all the pieces into an envelope. Make a note on it about any problems you had and add the name and age of the child.

4. Streamline production. Cut out two or more garments from the same pattern. Even if you don't make both of them immediately, you will at least have made a start on the next one. But in fact it hardly seems to take much longer to make two. Line up the processes and sew all the seams, all the sleeves, all the hems etc. This is also marvellous practice for you. Apply the same principle if you have more than one child, making something for each one.

5. Plan accessories at the same time: a purse, cap, bag, headband, apron, shoebag or toy.

6. Children love pockets. Even if the pattern doesn't include them they are easy to add, provided that you do it before the garment pieces are joined.

7. Put hanging loops on everything, including trousers — useful at home as well as school. Use pieces of tape, seam binding or ribbon.

8. Sew name tapes in where necessary. It is less of a chore than having to do it later.

9. When making outer clothes, build in strips of reflector tape.

10. Don't waste fabric; make frills and ruffles single not double, for example.

11. Keep all the scraps for patchwork, appliqué etc.

12. Get the child involved and learning simple sewing alongside you.

Techniques

When selecting the seams, edgings, openings etc., it is essential to remember that they must withstand laundering as well as strain and wear. In addition, remember the following points:

1. Construct clothes so that ironing will not be difficult.

2. Do not fit clothes too tightly; it is useful to be able to slip a sweater or T-shirt underneath.

3. Follow the sewing instructions found in various sections of this book but add an extra row of stitching for strength. Fasten off ends of thread very strongly.

4. Make use of bar tacks to strengthen ends of seams and openings.

5. Hand sewing is less strong than machining, so keep it to a minimum.

6. Avoid loose parts that flip such as wrapovers and facings; they should be stitched down.

7. Binding is a useful edge finish. It is strong, and contrasting fabric can be used.

8. If using Vilene/Pellon, make sure it is either enclosed or stitched in place.

9. Do not leave raw edges unfinished as the seam allowances will soon fray to nothing and seams will pull.

10. Avoid using shiny synthetic lining fabrics. Instead use cotton, brushed cotton or Viyella in outer clothes such as duffle coats and anoraks; use fine polyester cotton or lawn or even self fabric where yokes and other small areas are required to be double.

11. Use polyester or cotton-covered polyester-core thread for all seams. It is a good deal stronger than mercerized thread.

SAFETY

The question of safety is of paramount importance when choosing styles and fabrics for children.

There are a number of points to consider at the planning stage as well as during construction.

Fabric

A certain amount of fabric is available that is flame-retardant and this should be used for nightwear. However, dressing gowns are also a hazard and suitably treated fabrics for these are harder to find. Pyjamas are safer than nightdresses but remember that lace edgings, dressing gown cords etc. will probably burn even if the fabric merely smoulders. In homes where there are open fires or radiant heaters it is best to buy ready-made nightwear, making sure that it is labelled by the manufacturer as conforming to legal safety standards.

No fabric is completely fireproof. You should be careful even with outer clothes. Close-fitting garments are safest; loose ones create a chimney of air. Fabrics that are brushed or furry burn fast because of the air in the surface texture. Synthetic fibres do not, on the whole, flare up in the same way as some natural fibres such as cotton, but most of them melt and the molten substance causes burns. However, many fabrics are blends of various fibres and it is impossible to predict how they would burn. If you are planning long or full clothes that could be worn in winter it is worth testing the fabric. Buy pieces of several fabrics and, at home, hold small pieces over the sink and set light to them.

Avoid lacy or open fabrics; babies get fingers caught, and older children can get them caught on things. Avoid fabrics with loose fluffy fibres that can be inhaled.

Style

Make sure long skirts are not too long. Young girls find it difficult to cope with a long skirt on steps and stairs.

Avoid cords and ties at necklines and on hoods; use elastic or buttons.

Avoid loose panels, wide sleeves, long sash ends etc. Any of these could trip a child up, get caught in furniture or topple hot drinks.

Stitching

Hand-sewn hems are best avoided. They can easily be torn and become dangerous. Even a fallen hem on trousers could cause a child to trip.

Make sure buttons are firmly sewn. This is important for older children and essential for babies and toddlers who could pull them off and swallow them. Elastic must be stitched firmly and not allowed to become loose.

Make sure all sewing is secure and the garment is comfortable, with no loose straps to fall down.

PATTERNS

Choosing the size

Children do not come in standard sizes any more than adults, so the problems of pattern size and subsequent fitting are equally varied. If you also take into account that children grow, the problems are even more extensive.

You will know if your child is bigger or smaller, fatter or thinner than others the same age. A one-year-old baby can be the size of an average two-year-old but not be thought large. A little girl of eight or nine who is as slim as a six-year-old is lucky because she will probably be slim when she is an adult. At the back of the pattern catalogue there will be a chart giving measurements for each pattern size. You will find children's patterns in three categories: babies, toddlers and children. Adjustment in length is not difficult provided you remember to make it when cutting out the fabric. It makes sense to buy a pattern closest to the child's body width measurements so that at least shoulders and chest are correct and comfortable.

Remember that ease for movement will have been allowed for in your pattern. There is no need to buy the pattern a size larger unless the child is shooting up like a rocket or you have doubts about your ability to make the garment before he or she has grown substantially. If a garment is illustrated or described as full, close-fitting or loose, then that is what the pattern will be like.

Choose the size as follows and check the length before you cut out.

Babies. The pattern catalogue will show body weight for each size pattern and possibly an age guide. Selecting by weight has the advantage that the pattern will be big enough, although as with older children you should still check the length if the baby is already 'long'.

Toddlers. As soon as children start being active, they become slimmer and lose their baby roundness. Choose the pattern nearest to the chest size, checking length measurements before cutting out.

Children. With the lengthening of limbs, the patterns you buy may be different in style and from now on it is the length above and below the waist that is important rather than the overall size. If the child is particularly long in the body it will help if you make sure patterns for jumpsuits, dungarees, dresses etc. have a waist seam so that you can lengthen the pattern at that point before cutting out.

The catalogue and the pattern itself will show the chest size for each pattern and also the back neck to waist measurement for each size. Choose mainly by chest measurement unless the child is well below or above the average height for that age. If this is so, you may well get a better fit by selecting a different size.

Taking measurements

For both toddlers and children, measure the child around the chest, under the arms, with the tape straight and comfortably on the body over a vest or T-shirt.

Measure the back neck to waist at the position shown on the illustration, rounding up to the nearest ¼in (6mm).

Make a note of the measurements and take them with you when you go to buy the pattern.

Checking the pattern size

You will need some length measurements before cutting out. Depending on the temperament of the child you may do better if you measure existing clothes that fit, rather than wrestle with a writhing body. The position for taking the measurements is shown on the illustration.

Check the length of each pattern piece. Some measurements will be shown on the back of the pattern envelope and you can compare the child's measurements with those. With others, measure along the pattern piece at the seam edge but remember to subtract the seam and hem allowances as printed on the pattern.

Take the following measurements on both child and pattern. In addition check waist and hip width if you know the child is chubby.

Trousers and shorts, dresses with waist and skirts. Measure the side seam from waist to required length. Note that if pattern shows a high-waisted garment, measure the child from that position or check with waist position as printed on pattern.

Sleeves. Measure from underarm to required length along seam. Subtract seam and hem allowance when measuring pattern.

Adjusting the pattern

If the pattern is the correct length or longer, but you wish to build in more fabric, move on to *Allowing for Growth*, p. 120. If the pattern is too short, lengthen as follows, bearing these points in mind.

1. Always insert paper evenly across pattern, keeping grain arrows straight. In all cases, finish by re-drawing pattern edge in a smooth line and trimming off surplus paper.

2. Glue the pieces of paper together (or use adhesive tape); pins will fall out. Write the name of the child on the pattern and the date on which he or she was that size.

3. Remember that corresponding pieces such as facings will have to be lengthened too.

4. Buttonholes may need re-spacing. You will not need a longer zipper: simply move the stitching point to a new position.

Trousers and shorts. If the child is long in the leg add extra paper at the trouser hem, but if pattern is shaped, cut across it at 3in (8cm) above hem, spread the pieces and insert extra paper **(1)**.

For a tubby figure, add extra length by raising the waist edge of the pattern, adding extra paper **(2)**.

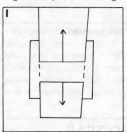
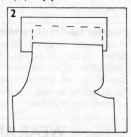

Skirt. If the pattern is straight, add extra required at hemline. If pattern is flared, cut straight across it at 3in (8cm) above hemline, spread the pieces and add extra paper.

Sleeve. Cut across pattern between wrist and elbow and insert extra paper.

Bodice (includes bib fronts etc.). Cut across back and front pattern 1¼–1½in (3–4cm) above waist edge, spread the pieces and insert paper.

FABRICS

Fabrics for children's clothes must be strong, washable and comfortable to wear. In addition, for your sake, it is best to avoid those that fray badly. Although white and pale colours are traditionally used for babies, most mothers opt for strong colours, both bright and dark, especially for school or daily wear.

Avoid open-weave, lacy, slippery and delicate fabrics and go for the ones that are robust. There is no need to spend a fortune; many of the most suitable fabrics are economically priced and children don't know the difference. Many fabrics are preshrunk during manufacture but if you are combining different fabrics or if a fabric was particularly low-priced, play safe by soaking or washing in plain water before sewing.

Read the section on *Safety*, p. 113, before choosing fabric, especially for nightwear. Consult *Fabrics*, p. 133, for details of the best way to handle the fabrics.

The following are suitable for children's clothes and are not difficult to sew.

Lightweight and cool. Calico, cambric, cheesecloth, cotton, crinkle cotton, eyelet, gingham, lawn, madras, percale, pique, poplin, polyester cotton, seersucker, voile.

Lightweight but soft and warm. Broadcloth, brushed cotton, brushed polyester, brushed viscose/rayon, chino, Clydella, cotton jersey, nylon jersey, polyester jersey, spun polyester, spun viscose/rayon, stretch towelling, Viyella, wool challis.

Heavier fabrics of various thicknesses. Blanket cloth, blazer cloth, brushed acrylic, cotton velvet, corduroy, denim, double knit, flannel, fur fabric, gaberdine, jersey and tracksuit jersey, melton, needlecord, proofed poplin, plastic fabrics, quilted fabrics, reversible cloth, sailcloth, suede fabric, ticking tweed, towelling, velour and jersey velour, velveteen, wool and wool coating.

WEAR AND TEAR

Repairs to children's clothes are the same as to adult clothes except that brighter contrasts and fun ideas can be used. However, it will make life easier if you build in some extra strength to areas of strain and wear by reinforcing the garment as you construct it.

Reinforcements

Sensible precautions such as machine-stitched hems and strong pockets are often forgotten when making clothes, especially if you want to practise your hand stitches. However, these reinforcements need not be clumsy. The hem on a little girl's lightweight party dress can be trimmed with lace or braid, or a frill or ruffle added with a narrow machined hem. Corners of pockets can be strengthened by placing a small folded piece of fabric on WS to stitch through when you sew the corners. Belt loops on a girl's dress often come off, tearing the fabric. Avoid this by stitching the belt to the dress across the front waistline; this also means she won't lose the belt.

You probably know which areas your children wear through. One benefit of making their clothes is that you can make those areas of double fabric, lengthening the life of the garment and saving yourself some mending later.

You can reinforce with another layer of garment fabric if it is suitable, eg. denim; otherwise use a piece of plain strong cotton or polyester cotton.

Knees. Cut out front trouser legs. Cut out reinforcement pieces the same width and shape to extend above and below the knee. Fold in and press horizontal edges on RS or zigzag them. Place pieces WS up on WS trouser leg and baste or pin. Stitch along each edge to attach to trouser. Make up trousers, including edges of reinforcement in seams. Upper and lower edges can be shaped if you wish. For further strength press iron-on Vilene/Pellon to RS of reinforcements before attaching to trousers. Another alternative is to add wadding/batting and quilt the area.

When the outer fabric wears to a hole either cover it with a patch or trim and turn in worn edges and stitch to reinforcement beneath.

Elbows. Cut round or oval pieces of fabric and zigzag the edge. Place RS down on WS sleeve and stitch around outer edge. These too can have wadding/batting sandwiched between garment and patch, and quilting worked over.

Seat of trousers. If school trousers habitually wear out at the seat, put an extra piece of the same fabric on the outside of each leg covering the area. Fold under and machine stitch all round. When outer fabric wears through, undo stitching and remove reinforcement to reveal unworn trousers underneath.

Yokes. Yokes of girls' dresses often look limp even if they do not wear out. Make the yoke double to add crispness as well as to make ironing easier. Cut out front and back yokes, cutting only to fold edge at opening and omitting facing. Stitch shoulder and side seams of both yokes. Place yokes RS together, match edges, shoulders and side seams and stitch around neckline and along fastening edge. Trim and snip edges as far as machine stitching. Turn so that all fabric is RS out, ease out stitched edges by rolling them between your fingers. Press. Baste around armhole edges and along lower edges. Continue making dress.

Patches

While making children's clothes, plan a pattern of decorative appliqué shapes or a picture, part of which will fall on the area that usually wears out. Stitch whatever seams are possible while still keeping garment flat. Press Bondaweb/ Wonderunder or iron-on interfacing to WS of each piece of appliqué and mark out required shapes. Stitch around shapes with a small zigzag and cut them out, cutting outside stitching. Arrange in position on garment. If pieces overlap, attach under sections first. Baste in position or hold with basting tape or, if Bondaweb/Wonder-Under is on the back, peel off paper and press in position. Stitch around outside edge with a medium size close zigzag to cover edge. Add any extra stitching to complete design. Pieces can also be padded and quilted before applying.

Ready-made coloured patches of suede and corduroy are useful to cut to shape for appliqué and also make a quick repair to a garment.

A cheaper alternative is to make your own patches. Spend a bit of time at your sewing session to make a stock of patches using various brightly coloured fabrics. Press Bondaweb/Wonder-Under to WS of piece of fabric. Draw various suitable shapes and stitch along line with a small zigzag. Cut out pieces, outside stitching. Do not remove backing paper. Stitch around outside edge with medium size close zigzag. Add any decorative stitching and put away for later use. When needed, peel off paper and press patch in position using a hot iron and a damp cloth. It will make repair jobs a lot less tedious if you let the child choose whether he wants you to attach the apple, elephant, train, football etc. And while you are doing it, why not add another fun shape somewhere else, even if there isn't another hole in the garment?

Trousers. Small slim trousers are very difficult to mend as they are too narrow to reach inside or slide on to the free arm of the machine. Attach patches using Bondaweb/ Wonderunder as described above or sew by hand using blanketstitch and thick thread or wool.

ALLOWING FOR GROWTH

There are various ways of building in extra length for use when it becomes necessary. Your choice depends on the style of garment. Remember that the extra fabric must be stitched up initially for safety.

Remember to buy extra fabric if adding length.

It is more difficult to allow for widthways growth as the garment would be bulky and lack style. However, if it looks as though this is going to be a problem, choose knits, as they can be worn for longer; also, consider styles with vertical seams that could later have contrasting fabric or braid inserted.

Trousers. 3–4in (8–10cm) additional hem can be allowed and turned up inside. In lightweight fabric, fold up the hem three times and stitch. Alternatively, make hem half depth and fold it back as a cuff. Secure cuff safely with bar tacks.

Additional rise can be allowed above the waist level of the trousers. Fold down a deep casing or hem and stitch two channels for elastic. Insert elastic in lower channel and when the child grows move it to top one.

Skirt. Straight skirts can have an extra 4–5in (10–13cm) added. This can be stitched as a three-fold hem, or it can be made into two or three flat tucks above the hem. Stitch tucks with a large straight machine stitch which can easily be withdrawn to release one tuck at a time.

Bodice. Lengthen the back and front pattern by cutting across and spreading the pieces as described under *Adjusting the pattern*, p. 117. Cut out in fabric, stitch the side seams and finish the bodice, then fold out the extra length above the waist in a tuck on the outside. Use a large machine stitch and withdraw it when necessary. For a more decorative effect, sew several small parallel tucks on RS.

Sleeves. If sleeves are to have cuffs or elastic, lengthen them by cutting pattern as described previously. Cut out fabric and stitch seams but make several small parallel tucks above lower edge before adding wrist finish. On boys' clothes this can be one wide tuck.

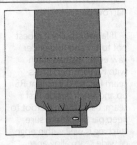

Straight sleeves of coats and shirts can be lengthened at hem and folded back to form a cuff. Secure with bar tacks.

Bibs. Cut the fabric longer and stitch the surplus in a flat tuck across finished bib or alternatively tuck it into skirt or trousers, joining at waist with topstitching that can be moved later.

Straps. Always cut straps long. Some of the surplus can be tucked into the back waist. You can also sew three buttons to front ends to be adjusted as necessary.

Remember to keep all the spare fabric for false hems, frills, ruffles and flounces to be added if necessary.

SEAMS

Seams form the skeleton: it is on them that the strength of children's clothes depend. The seams will be subject to alarming and unexpected strain, so where possible choose a type that involves two lines of stitching.

Fell seam. This is the most suitable of all seams for children's clothes, not only because it is strong but also because it is flat. Also called welt seam, flat-fell seam or double-stitched seam, it is suitable for all types of fabric.

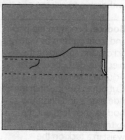

With pieces of fabric WS together, stitch on seamline. Long seams may need pinning first to prevent slippage, unless you have dual feed mechanism on your machine. Press both seam allowances toward back of garment. Lift seam allowances and trim lower one to ¼in (6mm). Fold under upper edge and tuck it under narrow one. Baste, press, and stitch along fold. The basting can be omitted on many fabrics. In fact, if you fold under and press the edge and stitch immediately, you can dispense even with pins. It will also help to keep seam flat if you stitch from the hem or wider part upward to the narrow part.

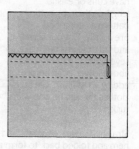

If fabric is bulky it is best not to try and fold under raw edge. Instead stitch with RS together, press seam flat, hold garment RS up and stitch beside first seam, using machine foot to keep parallel. Make sure stitching is well within edge of wide seam allowance beneath. If the fabric frays, finish edge with zigzag before working the final row of stitching.

On very fine fabrics or for baby clothes the seam can be sewn by hand if preferred, using running stitch and hemming.

Overlaid seam (or lapped seam). This can be used almost anywhere, but is particularly useful where gathers or tucks occur at yokes, waist seams, panels etc., and where careful matching is necessary. Suitable for all fabrics except possibly those that are very bulky or springy.

Fold under and press
seam allowance on upper
or ungathered edge. Baste
only if really necessary.
Overlap this edge onto
piece it is to join, matching
pressed edge to seamline.
Pin across seam at each end
to avoid stretching, then
insert several pins between.
Baste, remove pins and
stitch on RS close to fold

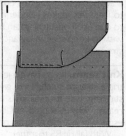

(1). Add a second row if required the width of the machine
foot away. If the fabric frays, trim and zigzag raw edges on
WS after working first row of stitching.

Alternatively, on soft fabrics, trim under layer of gathered
edge only, fold under upper edge twice, bringing it onto
machine stitches, and baste and hem to finish **(2)**.

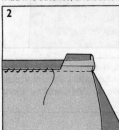

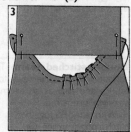

If lower section is gathered, pin at each end as described,
pull up gathering thread, even out gathers along seam; then
pin, baste and proceed as above **(3)**.

On baby clothes a decorative hand embroidery stitch can
be worked through all layers in place of machine stitching.

Open seam. Although not as strong as double stitched
seams, this one may have to be used on sleeves and narrow
trouser legs if you cannot reach inside once edges have
been joined. Suitable for all fabrics. Also known as a plain or
basic seam.

With fabric RS together
and edges even, stitch on
seamline. Press seam to
smooth stitching, then open
out fabric. Arrange it on
pressing surface WS up,
open seam allowances with
your fingers, pushing hard
on fabric. Press along seam
with tip of iron, opening
seam with your fingers in
front of iron. Press again. It

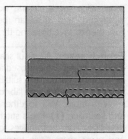

is advisable to zigzag raw edges even if fabric does not seem to fray; this makes laundering easier as edges are less likely to curl up. Topstitching can be added beside seamline if you wish to keep seam allowances flat, but it will not make seam stronger.

Knit seam. If you have a jersey stitch on your machine, eg. triple straight stitch, it will give you the strongest of all seam stitching. Use it on all knits and stretch fabrics. There is no reason why it should not be used on woven fabrics too, especially in areas of strain on tough fabrics such as denim.

With fabric RS together, stitch along seamline. Press seam open as described on previous page for *Open seam*. Raw edges of knits do not usually need to be zigzagged but trim seam allowances to ⅜in (1cm).

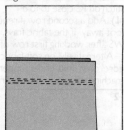

Double stitched seam. This is the alternative if you cannot do a special jersey stitch. Use on all knits and stretch fabrics and also as an alternative to open seam if extra strength is required.

With fabric RS together, stitch along seamline. On knits set your machine to a very slight zigzag, the setting only just off 0 if possible. This will allow some 'give' in the seam. If you cannot do this, use a straight stitch but pull fabric a little to stretch it as it goes under machine foot. This too has the effect of putting more thread into

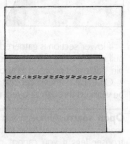

seam, which adds 'give'. Stitch seam again ¹⁄₁₆in (2mm) from first row, using same stitch. Press stitching, then press both seam allowances to one side. Woven fabrics should be zigzagged, and this can be worked over both edges together to save time and thread.

French seam. A useful seam for soft fabrics that fray, as the raw edges are enclosed and cannot be rubbed by wear or washing. Particularly suitable for baby clothes, nightwear and girls' dresses in fine fabrics.

With fabric WS together stitch halfway between edge and seamline **(1)**. Press stitching, then press both edges to one side. Trim both edges to ⅛in (3mm). Turn fabric over and press seam again to eliminate any crease or wrinkle.

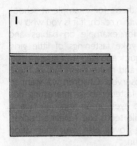

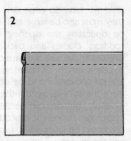

Fold fabric RS together, with seam along edge and press carefully with tip of iron. If fabric is springy, omit this pressing as it will have no effect. Baste seam below edge, then stitch ¼in (6mm) from edge using machine foot as a guide **(2)**. Check distance between machine needle and outside edge of foot before working this second row. If it is substantially more than ¼in (6mm) adjust seam accordingly or perhaps move needle position.

In any case it is worth checking the seam itself before stitching. Hold it up to the light and you will see where raw edges are in relation to line of basting. Machine stitching must fall outside raw edges.

Remove basting and press seam to one side.

This seam can be worked using hand running stitch instead of machining; this method is particularly suitable for baby clothes.

Narrow seam. Similar to the two seams above and useful on fabrics that fray. Suitable for all fabrics including knits.

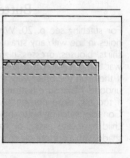

With fabric RS together, stitch along seamline with a straight stitch or, on knits, slight zigzag or knit stitch. Trim seam allowances together to ¼in (6mm) and zigzag over them. Press seam to one side.

Note: Where two bulky seams meet and you are about to make another seam, either press the matching seam allowances in opposite directions to reduce bulk, or move them slightly apart.

FASTENINGS

Fastenings selected for children's clothes should be simple, reliable, securely attached, and strong in themselves. If the child will have to cope with them, for example at school, they must also be large and within reach. If it is you who will be operating the opening, for example on babies' and toddlers' clothes and back yoke fastenings of little girls' dresses, make sure they are quick and easy, not fiddly.

Use a variety of fasteners and make them fun, as there are no conventions to be observed. Children will want to learn the skills involved if the fastener looks interesting. For example, buttons can be the eyes on an appliqué face, a zipper can represent crocodile teeth and reveal a pocket, ties could be laces on boxing gloves. Use your imagination and the sewing will be more fun.

Buttons

For attaching see p. 23. Choose them big and bright. Keep to flat buttons; avoid fancy or dome-shaped buttons and all metal buttons except covered blazer buttons. Always make a good shank; buttons are very difficult to fasten if sewn flat. Use polyester thread or button thread, doubled and waxed. On play clothes and tough fabric reinforce by adding a piece of tape, folded and placed on underside of garment. Always insert a strip of interfacing or an extra piece of fabric between garment and facing to take the strain. If possible allow for growth by attaching an extra button, or even two, when making the garment. This can be done on waistbands and dungaree and pinafore straps.

Buttonholes

For stitching see p. 20. Wherever possible make button-holes in line with any strain of movement, ie. *horizontal* on shirts, blouses, dresses, nightwear; running *along* a cuff or waistband not across it; and *along* a strap or hood fastening. If they run the other way the buttons will too easily come undone. Make sure buttonholes are firm and the right size. If too big, close one end with oversewing or a bar tack. Consider stitching buttonholes in a contrasting yarn for the child to locate easily, or having every button a different shade with a buttonhole to match.

Loops

Thread loops are not a good idea except on baby clothes. Rouleau tubing loops can be used occasionally singly or in pairs but long rows will be too much to cope with for both you and the child. Tape or seam binding can be used, folded to a point, if one big loop is required. A bright shade will make it a more interesting fastening. Cord can also be used, although a very long shank is then required on the button, which makes it likely to come undone easily. For loops on outer clothes and duffle coats use braid, using two pieces on top of each other and stitching along edges.

Attach loops firmly by stitching across them twice before attaching garment facing, binding or other edge finish. If loop is not set in garment seam, stitch in place on garment's RS. Either fold under ends and stitch all round again for strength and neatness or cover loop ends with appliqué shapes and stitch all round. You can have fun here with contrasting textures such as leather and plastic as well as with colour and design.

Toggles

Children love these and they come in a variety of shapes and sizes. Confine them to older children's outer clothes as they do not form a firm fastening and are dangerous for toddlers to fall on.

Ties

Make ties from fabric or from tape, seam binding or ribbon. They may be the cheapest fastening of all but although they look pretty on babies, and little girls' dresses and nightwear, ties are not always the best choice. Never use them as neckline drawstrings on any garment. Attach them by sewing firmly across end or by inserting end in garment seam. On baby clothes do not attach them where they can be sucked or chewed. Make sure there is no danger of them coming off and being swallowed. Never leave overlong ends that could become entangled around any part of the baby.

On toddlers' clothes apply the same safety rules, making sure there are no ends to trip them up. Remember that ties take time to undo if clothes have to come off in a hurry.

For older children ties can be used more extensively but still keep the ends short and do not put them on school clothes until child has learnt to tie a bow.

Hooks

For attaching see p. 31. On the whole, hooks, apart from very tiny ones, are not a good idea on baby clothes, because they would be uncomfortable. However, they are a cheap, strong fastening for older children's clothes. Use large size hooks and metal eyes or bars; thread loops are difficult to locate and the fabric tends to become worn. Use hooks only as a front fastening: children will not be able to cope with them at the back. Large flat trouser hooks with bars are good on waists, as they are firm. They also have the advantage of being the same as on adult trousers, which can be important to little boys. Attaching additional hooks for growth is not a good idea because they will tend to catch in things. A trouser waistband can be made too long, with elastic through it, which can be removed when the child grows. Another good alternative is to attach an adjustable fastener comprising one flat hook with a corresponding part containing three or more sockets.

Snaps

For attaching see p. 33. Apart from buttons, snaps are probably the best fastening of all children's clothes. For you and the children they are quick to undo, and children enjoy learning to use them. Apart from neck openings on baby clothes, choose large size snaps that will be easy to find. Avoid plastic snaps as they are too fiddly. Where several are required, snaps on tape are a good idea.

Decorative snap fasteners

Although a heavier fastening, these are even better for children's clothes. They are available in packs which include a tool for attaching them, and there is a variety of metal and plastic tops to match or contrast with the fabric. There is no sewing involved, which is an encouragement for beginners. Decorative snap fasteners are suitable for most garments and any position. If they have a disadvantage it is that if you misjudge the position, there is no second chance as there is with stitched fastenings.

'D' rings

These are a good quick-release fastener for straps on toddlers' clothes and they automatically adjust the garment to size. Make sure straps are safely attached to garment. Apart from metal, 'D' rings are available in bright shades to match decorative snap fasteners.

Buckles

For safety, use only plastic buckles without prongs on clothes for young children. This does not make a secure fastening, so a snap would also have to be added.

Velcro tape

For attaching see p. 36. A good choice for practically all openings except necklines of baby clothes. Even young children can line up the corresponding parts and press to close. It is also a useful fastener on things like pockets, hats, hoods, belts and bags as well as on nursery and bedroom accessories. Always use sufficient length, 1½–2in (4–5cm) on waistbands, and use Spot-Ons/Velcoin fasteners in pairs for strength, in case the two pieces are not lined up accurately by the child. Use Velcro tape only on openings that remain closed in wear, or the hook side will catch other clothes. Remember to close before washing or it will collect fluff from fabrics.

Zippers

The great value of the zipper for children's clothes is that it is easy for them to learn to use, except for the separating zipper which takes more time. The zipper is quick to open, makes a secure fastening and is the best choice for long openings. Insert it at the front so that it can be reached. In the main, avoid lightweight zippers with small slide pulls; go for the medium and chunky types.

It is important to stitch accurately, keeping fabric edges well away from the teeth, because children will not be checking before fastening the zipper.

Covered zipper (or lapped zipper). Not the easiest method but a useful one because the zipper need not be a perfect match. The method is used on trousers, skirts and dresses. There will be a sufficiently wide seam allowance on your pattern to cover a lightweight zipper but others will require a total of ¾–1¼in(2–3cm). Check before cutting out fabric and add extra if necessary.

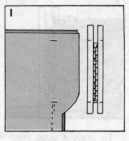

Baste seam as far as base of zipper section. Place closed zipper beside seam with upper edge of slider even with seamline at upper edge. Don't worry if tapes extend beyond fabric, they will be trimmed later. With zipper in this position and using a fabric marking pen, mark a point on seam even with zipper bottom-stop. Make two marks, one on each seam allowance, at top of seam even with top of slider. Make corresponding marks on zipper tapes **(1)**. When inserting a zipper in a dress with a waist seam, also mark tapes at waist level to provide useful matching points. These marks ensure zipper will be in correct position and also stop you stretching the fabric.

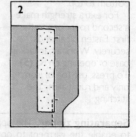

Stitch seam to mark and fasten off. Fold under and press upper seam allowance – the one that will cover the zipper. If fabric is springy, baste it back in position. If it is lightweight or soft, cut a strip of light iron-on interfacing and press it to garment under seam allowance, with one edge along crease, before basting **(2)**. Alternatively, press a piece of soft Fold-a-Band in position with central perforations along the crease.

With garment RS toward you, fold back the pressed edge. On the underside fold under raw edge of remaining seam allowance, *not* along seamline but ⅛–¼in (3–6mm) nearer raw edge (depending on thickness of fabric). If you have not previously marked the seamline it helps to do so now, making dots using a fabric marking pen. Fold under seam allowances and press. Baste if necessary.

Attach basting tape to both zipper tapes on RS. Place zipper beside the edge just pressed and remove basting tape covering. Place zipper under garment edge matching corresponding marks. Press fabric in position over tape. Stitch close to edge of fabric from end to end of zipper tape **(3)**. Use machine stitching or hand backstitch. For strength stitch again ⅛in (3mm) away.

Remove covering tape from second side of zipper, overlap prepared wide edge onto zipper, matching edge fold to seamline underneath, *not* to stitching or teeth. The wide edge will completely cover the zipper area. Press fabric in place along zipper, matching marks at the top.

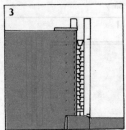 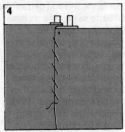

To prevent edge from moving, use large oversewing stitches to catch fold to garment beneath. Mark a straight line for stitching the zipper ⅛in (3mm) from the teeth, using a fabric marking pen and feeling the teeth **(4)**. Mark across the bottom below the stop. Stitch along the line, preferably from bottom to top.

For extra strength make a second row close to the first. Fasten off all ends securely. Work a bar tack at base of opening on RS **(5)**. To press, use toe of iron only and run it along the stitching.

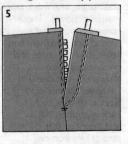

Separating zipper. The zipper itself is visible and is used to enable the garment to open up completely. On loose garments the zipper may not reach the hem. It is easy to sew, especially if the garment edges are complete. In fact it is worth completing the edges with binding, facings, lining etc. if you have not done so. If for some reason you cannot do so, turn under and press the garment edges and baste. Complete the garment hem with ribbing, elastic, stitched hem etc., and also the neck edge if possible. Take care to make the garment edges exactly equal in length.

Place closed zipper beside garment edge with both ends in position. If zipper is shorter than opening it does not matter – adjust the position slightly. Make several pairs of corresponding matching marks on garment and zipper tapes. If neck edge of garment is complete, fold zipper tapes back at right

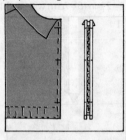

angles and stitch. Press lengths of basting tape in position on RS of zipper tapes. Separate two halves of zipper. Working on one side at a time, remove covering tape, place zipper underneath garment edge, match marks and press in position. Stitch beside teeth by hand or machine, and again 1/16in (2mm) away. Fasten ends securely. Stitch yet again for a short distance at bottom of zipper through reinforced non-fraying end of tape.

Even hems (or slot zipper). If edges of fabric are to meet along centre of zipper teeth, stitch seam, then stitch along where zipper is to go. Press open entire seam. Place closed zipper beside seam with slider in correct position at top of opening alongside collar, facing, binding etc. Make two or three pairs of matching marks on zipper and seam. Place basting tape on RS of each zipper tape. Remove covering tape and place RS down on seam allowances, lining up teeth along seam. Press in position. Stitch alongside zipper from RS of garment. If you need a guideline make a row of dots with a fabric marking pen, feeling position of teeth beneath and marking stitching line at least 1/8in (3mm) away. If possible stitch from base to top on each side without stitching across bottom, which can cause a bulge.

Visible zipper. This method means there is little chance of the child catching fabric in the zipper; you don't have to have a seam to put it in and it relieves you of anxiety about covering the teeth.

If there is a seam in the garment, stitch as far as base of opening and press open. Fold back seam allowances far enough to make a gap between the edges equal to width of zipper teeth. This measurement will obviously depend on type of zipper selected. For accuracy mark fold lines on RS using tailor's chalk or fabric marking pen. Press. At base of opening snip at an angle and fold under point to form a neat opening. Baste edges back if fabric is springy.

If there is no seam, draw a line the length of zipper teeth, cut on line and out at an angle at bottom. Fold under edges and bottom triangle to produce a gap equal to width of teeth **(1)**. Alternatively, if this would give a raw edge too narrow to fold under, make a faced slit. Cut a strip of fabric 2–2¾in (5–7cm) wide and 1¼in (3cm) longer than zipper.

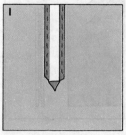
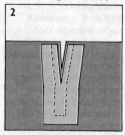

Fold lengthwise and press. Place strip RS down on RS of garment, matching crease to marked line. Stitch ⅛in (3mm) from crease along each side and across bottom. This will make a gap ¼in (6mm) wide. If your zipper is larger or smaller, adjust measurement. Cut between stitching lines **(2)** and out to corners at bottom. Roll strip to WS and press edges.

Place zipper beside opening and make several pairs of matching marks with fabric pen. Place a strip of basting tape on RS of each zipper tape. Remove covering tape, place zipper under garment edges and press in position with edges beside teeth. Stitch all around, close to edge and again ⅛in (3mm) away.

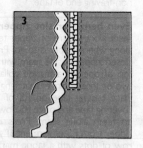

Alternatively, work one row of stitching, then stitch braid, ric-rac or ribbon on top **(3)**.

FABRICS

Your satisfaction, or otherwise, with a particular item of clothing is directly related to the suitability of the fabric. Choosing fabrics to sew with is not easy: even if you have considerable experience, you cannot be quite certain what the finished garment will be like in every degree.

FABRIC CHOICE

When choosing fabric, bear in mind the points listed below. In addition, be guided by the ready-made clothes you have and the fabrics from which they are made. For example, if a particular shirt is hot or prickly to wear, look at the label and remember to avoid that type of fabric. If you have a dress that is always slipping off its hanger, that type of fabric will slip around when you try to sew it. You will also learn something about wear and creasing by examining clothes that you have had for a while.

Given that you will obviously select a fabric that appeals to you and suits you when you drape it on yourself in front of the store mirror, consider also the following:

Design

If you are a beginner avoid checks and stripes, except those that are narrow and evenly spaced. Also avoid any design that will need careful matching or placing for a good effect. This includes large and one-way printed fabrics. Play safe by choosing plains, nearly-plains and small printed designs. Always have a look at the range of fabric that is available before buying your paper pattern so that you have something in mind when looking through the pattern catalogue.

Check the total weight of the amount you will be using, especially if it is for a child or elderly person or if the fabric is thick. This may also be an important point for an evening gown or a wedding dress.

Draping quality

Even if you have not bought your pattern, you will know whether you are looking for a crisp fabric that will pleat or a soft one that will gather. Drape the fabric and hold it as it will look when made up. Make sure it is sufficiently pliable for your needs.

Handling

On the whole, shiny fabrics are not easy for a beginner to sew except as very small items. Keep to matt fabrics, but also look at the construction. If the fabric is loosely woven you may have a problem with fraying yarn ends. Look at the cut edge and gently feel it between your fingers. If any yarns come loose you will know that it will fray easily when you cut it. This is something that can be overcome, but beginners tend to be slow and to handle fabric more, which makes the problem worse for them.

Purpose

Your ready-made clothes will have given you some guidance, so consider this aspect when choosing the type of fabric. You should opt for a knit fabric for clothes that need to expand for comfort. This will allow children to be active, maternity clothes to be free of restriction, and sports clothes to remain comfortable without allowing perspiration to cool on the skin.

Wear

Finally, consider whether the fabric you like will last as long as you hope. Chiffon is fine for evening gowns, denim and cord are excellent for items in daily use, cotton is cool and comfortable for shirts. These are all points you will have discovered from existing clothes. If you break the rules, do it knowingly. By all means make satin trousers and a lace shirt – this is one of the exciting benefits of home sewing – but beware that their life may be limited.

TYPES OF FABRIC

Some fabrics are composed of 100% cotton or silk or wool etc., but many are blends of two or more ingredients, often a combination of natural and synthetic raw material. These blends are a feature of modern textiles, giving us the best of both worlds – the softness and resilience of cotton, silk, wool and linen with the uncrushable strength of nylon, polyester and acrylic. Look at the label: whatever is listed as having the highest percentage will be predominant. For example, polyester is incredibly tough but a cotton fabric containing only 10–15% polyester will be no more hard-wearing than 100% cotton, although it will crease a little less. A 50/50 or 60/40 combination will be very hard-wearing and will crease a lot less. A fabric containing 90% wool will look and feel exactly like all-wool: the other 10% may be a purely decorative fleck or novelty effect.

Lightweight matt wovens

Beginners should choose fabrics in this group as being the least trouble to handle.

Includes: Cotton, Swiss cotton, cotton modal, cotton crepon, seersucker, gingham, madras, batiste, lawn eyelet, polyester cotton.

Machine needle size 80 (11). Medium stitch.
Seams: French, open or welt.
Press: Hot/steam iron.
Launder: Hot wash.

Medium-weight wovens

Also easy to handle and suitable for beginners.

Includes: Corduroy, needlecord, soft denim, poplin, polyester cotton, linen, woven polyester, woven viscose/rayon, brushed cotton, brushed viscose/rayon, wool challis,

Machine needle size 90 (14). Medium to long stitch.
Seams: Open or welt.
Press: Warm – hot/steam, depending on content.
Launder: Hot wash cottons, linen and polyester cotton. Warm hand wash wool.

Heavy-weight wovens

A little heavy for beginners.

Includes: Canvas, heavy cord, heavy denim, coating, proofed poplin, heavy cotton and linen, gaberdine, sailcloth, heavy glazed cotton.

Machine needle size 90–100 (14–16); or 90 (14) jeans needle. Long stitch.
Seams: Welt, open, topstitched.
Press: Hot/steam iron.
Launder: Hot wash.

Slippery wovens

Should be avoided by beginners. All these fabrics fray.

Includes: Silk, crepe de Chine, Thai silk, raw silk, shantung, polyester crepe de Chine, polyester satin, silk satin, silk Jacquard, polyester Jacquard, taffeta, acetate satin.

Machine needle size 90 (14). Medium to long stitch.
Put paper or Stitch-n-Tear beneath if fabric wrinkles.
Seams: Open, topstitched.
Press: Cool iron, no moisture, protect RS with dry cloth.
Launder: Hot wash polyester; dry clean silk; warm wash acetate (do not spin). It may be safe to hand wash silk; test by washing a measured square first. Dry, press and re-measure.

Lightweight knits

Except for slippery fabrics these are not difficult to sew.

Includes: Cotton jersey, T-shirt fabric, polyester jersey, acrylic knit, cotton modal jersey, lacy knit.

Machine needle size 70 (9) ball-point. Medium stitch.
Seams: Knit or double stitched.
Press: Warm/steam iron; light pressure, do not move until cold.   Launder: Warm wash.

Heavy knits

May be referred to as double knits. These are usually easy to sew and a good choice for beginners in simple styles.

Includes: Track suit jersey, velour, acrylic knit, brushed acrylic knit, jersey velour, triacetate velour, poodle or loop knit, pile knits, stretch towelling.

Machine needle size 90–100 (14–16). Long stitch.

Seam: Knit or double stitched, topstitched.

Press: Warm/steam iron; light pressure. Do not move until cold.

Launder: warm wash.

Sheers

Very fine and transparent. Not easy to sew, even for people with experience. The easiest ones are those made from cotton.

Includes: Silk chiffon, polyester chiffon, organdie, organza, cotton voile, polyester voile, polyester georgette, Robia voile, French voile, ninon, muslin/lawn, nylon, net, tulle, veiling, tricot.

Machine needle size 70 (9). Small stitch.

Seams: French, narrow.

Press: Cool/steam iron.

Launder: Warm-hot wash, but test for shrinkage first, especially chiffon and georgette.

PRESSING FABRIC

Whether bought or made at home, clothes should be cared for to give them maximum life and obtain value for money.

Most garments look better for a press after they have been laundered. Once you have learnt the necessary skills it can be a matter of some pride that your clothes are immaculate. Don't think your clothes are unworthy of this attention – even patches will look more professional if you press them after sewing them.

Equipment

The equipment for pressing is no problem. Results will depend partly on the skill you acquire.

Iron. A steam iron is easiest to use and always produces good results. Most fabrics need moisture applied as well as heat and a steam iron supplies both together. Never leave water in the iron between sessions. If possible avoid tap water. Most stores sell filter bottles or crystals for use with steam irons; follow the instructions for use. Keep the sole plate of the iron spotless by using an iron cleaner on it whenever scorch marks or traces of adhesive from iron-on products appear.

Ironing board. Pressing without a board is difficult, but large areas and flat unshaped seams can be pressed on a blanket or sheet arranged on the kitchen worktop. If you haven't an ironing board this is a good substitute. The ironing board enables you to slide tubular items on it and revolve them without creasing. The shaped end is for pushing into shoulders and armholes.

Sleeve board. Although a tool of the professional, the sleeve board is very useful for small shaped areas and for children's clothes.

Cloth. A pressing cloth is important. It can be used dry, covering the fabric to prevent direct contact between the iron and the fabric; occasionally necessary to prevent shine. Used damp and well wrung-out, the cloth is placed over the fabric to provide additional moisture; often required when setting creases and pleats and when pressing tough fabrics. The best type of pressing cloth is a yard or metre of muslin/lawn. Thicker fabric will hold too much water and make the garment wet — which can have disastrous results.

Seam roll. Sophisticated padded shapes can be bought to help with pressing small tubular areas, but a simple seam roll can be made by folding a towel and sliding it into sleeves, etc. Press garment, revolving whole sleeve, remove towel and shake sleeve once to cool fabric. If a firmer seam roll is required, put a rolled-up magazine inside towel.

How to press

Whether pressing clothes after laundering, revitalizing a worn garment, or setting the fabric in its new seamed position when sewing, remember the rules:

1. Set the iron according to the lowest heat required for the fabric, or set within the steaming area on the dial.
2. When using a damp cloth have the iron slightly hotter in order to penetrate the cloth.
3. Press WS first, then turn to RS and press again; but protect if necessary by covering with a dry cloth.
4. Allow plenty of time and don't hurry. Manipulate the tip of the iron rather than glide it aimlessly.
5. Allow the fabric to cool and dry. Put garments and partly made garments on hangers.

After laundering press in sequence as follows:

Pressing a shirt or blouse

1. Under side of collar; upper side of collar.
2. Edge of sleeve opening, inside cuff and outside cuff of one of the sleeves.

3. Fold sleeve along seam and smooth out. Press along seam. Press from seam across sleeve almost to crease. Press wrist tucks flat. For gathers, turn iron and insert point in and out of gathers.

4. Turn sleeve over, smooth and press from seam almost to crease. Press tucks or gathers. For shirt, press along sleeve crease. For blouse, open out sleeve and arrange with unpressed area down the middle. Smooth fabric and press centre of sleeve. Repeat steps 2, 3 and 4 on second sleeve.

5. Slide shoulder onto end of ironing board. Press right sleeve head and yoke, centre back of yoke and left sleeve head and yoke.

6. Press WS of buttonhole band, followed by RS. Press between buttons on WS followed by RS.

7. Slide body onto ironing board. Arrange right front edge on board, press beside band up to yoke and entire area that is flat on board. Revolve shirt away from you to avoid creasing. Press each side of side seam, revolve again and press half the back. Continue until pressing is complete. Put shirt on hanger or alternatively fasten buttons, fold sleeves onto back, fold in sides even with side of collar and fold into three to stack.

Pressing a skirt

With the exception of cotton skirts, a damp pressing cloth will probably be needed.

1. With skirt inside out, press lining.

2. Open zipper. Slide skirt waist onto ironing board and press over lining below waistband. Also press waistband.

3. Turn skirt RS out. Slide waist onto ironing board. Press area below waist then press waistband.

4. Slide skirt on to board, hem first, including lining if it is attached. Press up to zipper on each side. Close zipper. Move skirt a little way off ironing board and smooth out lower skirt area. Press each part using iron firmly on damp cloth without sliding. Revolve skirt away from you. Press until complete.

Pleats. Leave pleats until last, having pressed pleated area along with skirt. Press each pleat separately or two together if close. Fold into position. If weight of skirt drags pleat open, put a chair beneath ironing board to support skirt. Alternatively, if you have a sleeve board use this for pleats. Use pressing cloth folded double as more moisture will be required. Apply iron firmly two or three times on each part of crease. Remove cloth and immediately bang in the steam. Professionals use a wooden pressing block but a good substitute is the back of a clothes brush or a book, or even a smooth block of wood. Slap it smartly down and leave it there for several minutes or until fabric has cooled. If skirt is linen, iron over fabric after removing cloth and before applying block. If your book or block is smaller than length of pleat, hold pleat closed at hem with a pin and press upper part of pleat. When cool, remove pin and press hem, leaving block in position for some time.

Pin pleat flat or insert a couple of loose basting stitches to hold it. Move skirt round and press next pleat. Continue until complete. Put into a skirt clip and hang up immediately.

Pressing trousers

1. Press fly extension.

2. Slide trouser waist onto ironing board and press each side of zipper. Revolving the trousers, press area below waistband.

3. Press waistband.

4. With trouser leg folded, press inside leg area up to and around crotch. Repeat with second leg.

5. Holding trousers by hems, arrange so that old crease marks are at outer edges. If you have no marks to go by, a good trouser shape is one where inside leg seams are ⅜in (1cm) to front of trouser rather than even with seams at outside leg. Lay trousers along pressing surface, fold back upper leg and smooth out leg still on ironing board.

6. Begin at hem at front edge and press across leg, using iron firmly over a damp cloth. Place iron down two or three times in each place, working across leg to back. Move up leg a little way and repeat. Continue as far as possible. This has set trouser creases. Use a pressing block on the creases after removing the damp cloth, leaving block in position until fabric is quite cold. If necessary, press along crease a second time.

7. Loosely fold over pressed section of leg and carefully move trousers so that you can press up as far as crotch seam. Turn leg right over and press outside part. It will need very little attention if pressing has been done well up to this point.

8. Finish by pressing front crease right up to waist level and back crease almost as far as waist.

9. Unroll upper leg and lift trousers up holding them by the hems. Turn them over and prepare second leg to be pressed, loosely folding pressed one out of the way.

10. Press second leg. Hang trousers over bar of a hanger or by hems on a clip.

Pressing sewing techniques

Press fabric before and after stitching.

Stitching. Press every row of stitching as you make it. This will smooth out seam and help to embed thread in fabric.

Seams. After pressing stitching, open out fabric and slide iron alongside seam, under seam allowances. Press seam allowances in required direction.

Edges. Edges to be folded under and machine stitched are best pressed to provide a sharp edge on which to stitch. It also helps to press folded edges to be hand sewn.

On edges that are to be turned RS out, collar, cuffs etc., press stitching and trim edges before turning, then ease out corners using point of a bodkin. Roll seam at edge and press very carefully with tip of iron, pressing again to correct if you make a mistake. Press again along entire edge.

Darts. Press stitching first, open out fabric and arrange it WS up on ironing board. Make sure dart lies straight, with point even with end of board so that shape of fabric beyond point will not be pressed flat.

Hems. Press fold at garment edge and press hem depth; never press over stitched edge or an imprint will appear on outside of garment.

Pleats. Press firmly and leave undisturbed until fabric is quite cold. On all except cotton fabrics, bang in the steam using a pressing block. See p. 138 for details.

Gathers. After stitching a gathered seam, press along seam allowance with gathers uppermost, allowing iron to rest briefly on stitching. Turn RS out with gathers extending and press by sliding tip of iron in and out of gathers, holding fabric taut.

Decorative stitching. Embroidery satin stitch, buttonholes etc. Press on WS only. Embroidery can be raised by arranging a towel on the pressing surface into which the design can sink.

INDEX

INDEX